I

Dr. Nicholas Muteti's book is a powerful story of cross-cultural evangelism. In his book, he shares his own story of reaching across cultural and ethnic boundaries to share the gospel of the Lord Jesus Christ. In his retelling of his own personal story, he forms the basis of a belief that God's people need to worship together, not in separate racial and ethnic groups.

He powerfully points out the spiritual change that is necessary if true reconciliation is going to occur between racial and ethnic groups. He speaks of the power of the gospel and the power of the cross to break down barriers and build bridges into better relationships.

His story is a story of changed lives and of gospel intention in seeing people recognize the lordship of Christ and follow the commands of Christ in worship, discipleship, and ministry.

I commend Dr. Muteti's book to you and pray it will be an encouragement to you as it was to me.

—**Frank S. Page,** PhD
President and Chief Executive Officer
Southern Baptist Convention

I have never known a more courageous man than my friend Dr. Nicholas Muteti. His testimony of crossing tribal enemy lines to preach the gospel to the Maasai people of his native Kenya is one of the most inspiring stories I have ever heard. His courage remains undaunted as he now stands as a Christian leader in America. It's no surprise, then, that a man like Brother Nicholas would courageously address a hard subject, segregation in churches. He tackles a tough issue with grace and fearlessness, and provides biblical answers that every Christian needs to hear."

—**Dr. Stephen Rummage,** Senior Pastor
Bell Shoals Baptist Church, Brandon, Florida

Dr. Nicholas Muteti has strong convictions regarding the authority of Scripture. In this book he boldly proclaims that scripture is the truth that releases the power of God to change hard hearts of stone. Attitudes that created the culture of segregation in our churches can be changed through the preaching of the Word, personal counseling, discipleship, and shepherding the flock. The "culture of heaven" on earth is his goal. His passion is to see all believers looking beyond the color of human skin to see each person the way we will be seen in heaven. Then we will worship in churches with colorful congregations. I commend my brother for sharing part of his life story in this very interesting book. I appreciate his passion to see racial barriers dissolved in our churches in the same way God worked to unite the Maasai and Kamba tribes of Kenya.

—**Dr. Allan Blume**
Editor/President, *Biblical Recorder*
News Journal of the Baptist State
Convention of North Carolina

It is obvious that when we step into heaven, we will not all be from the same background or ethnic culture, nor will we have the same skin color. But to witness and observe many religious groups today, you would believe that statement to not be true. Brother Nicholas addresses a subject that is not easily broached in our culture today, but needs to be. His book is concise and necessary for our modern-day church and we need to listen to his words and wisdom.

—**Dr. C.J. Bordeaux,** Senior Pastor
Gorman Baptist Church,
Durham, North Carolina
First Vice President,
Baptist State Convention of North Carolina

Dr. Nicholas Muteti writes with the passion of an evangelist and the heart of a pastor when it comes to the subject of racial segregation in the church. Drawing from a strong biblical foundation, and the unique perspective of someone raised in Africa and educated in America, Dr. Nicholas Muteti sounds a clarion call for revival and renewal in the church. It is the author's conviction that real revival will elude the church until she repents and embraces the unity that is found in Christ.

—Dr. Frank R. Lewis, Senior Pastor
First Baptist Nashville, Tennessee

Dr. Muteti has tackled one of the most pressing problems in the church today—segregation. When others had their heads in the sand, he was not afraid to confront a volatile racial issue that causes disunity in the church. Using both biblical imperatives and gripping personal experiences, he captured the essence of the volatile and far-reaching problem of a segregated religion by comparing it to the resolution of tribal hatred among the Maasai and Kamba people in his native Kenya. "What has happened to these two tribes can happen to any people group around the world." Dr. Muteti challenges pastors as well as all Christians to have a radical heart change. He believes that we cannot force segregation in churches; we must have teachable and willing hearts to effect change. Since 90 percent of American churches are segregated, following Jesus' example of unconditional love, becoming true disciples, and focusing on evangelism are the keys to overcoming partiality and prejudice in the church. Dr. Muteti boldly asserts that "a born-again person should be color-blind." He says: "We cannot segregate ourselves and still be a Bible-believing people." Calling all of us to experience the joy of diversity, he uses powerful examples to debunk conventional wisdom and long-held myths about segregated worship. His most convincing argument is that our hearts are not right. Our attitude toward a segregated worship hour will only be affected when we begin to possess a shepherd's heart.

Dr. Muteti is like a modern day Alex de Tocqueville. The Frenchman came to this country in the mid-1800s to discover the essence of democracy in America. He revealed things about race relations that the American culture could not see for itself. Dr. Muteti came to America from Kenya expecting to see a unified church under the leadership of the Holy Spirit, only to be surprised at its underlying disunity, prejudice, and racial division. Shocked by our situation and courageous enough to address the problem, he made it his goal to show us a better way, and that way, amazing as it may seem, is to have a heart operation and be more like Christ.

Reading this book makes me feel a bit red-faced. A young boy in Kenya marched seven miles to an almost sure death to confront discrimination between tribes. We walk the other way rather than admitting that there is a segregation problem in Southern Baptist churches in America. We have taken a huge step, though, since the initial draft of Dr. Muteti's book, and I am proud to say our new President of the Southern Baptist Convention is Dr. Fred Luter, an African-American. His election as president could mean that Dr. Muteti's challenge will be the harbinger of change that throws light on the problem and causes a groundswell of enthusiasm to fix it.

Years ago, on vacation in Washington, DC, with Dr. Muteti, his wife, Joyce, and their children, we toured Arlington National Cemetery. Jimmy, the youngest son of Nicholas and Joyce, grew tired from the walk. Without even giving it a thought, I tossed him up on my shoulders and carried him from the parking lot to JFK's gravesite. Many were walking back, having already seen the attractions. After a while I noticed almost everyone staring at me carrying young Jimmy. Then I realized it must have been unusual to see a black child having fun on the shoulders of a white man in Washington, DC. We must learn in the church today not only to worship together, but also to build inter-racial relationships that feel natural and comfortable. Why? Well, because, as Dr. Muteti so aptly puts it in his book, God wants it that way. Heaven will not be segregated!

—**Dr. John Reale,** Senior Pastor
Staunton Baptist Church
Huddleston, Virginia

12/6/2014

For Bro. Mike + Sister Erin,
Let's Unite the
Church, the Community, the
World and All People
for Christ!?
God bless you!

SEGREGATION IN CHURCHES

SEGREGATION IN CHURCHES

PROVIDING GOD'S ANSWER TO SOLVE THE DILEMMA

DR. NICHOLAS M. MUTETI

WinePressPublishing
Great Books, Defined.

ISBN 13: 978-1-4141-2405-6
ISBN 10: 1-4141-2405-8
Library of Congress Catalog Card Number: 2012911330

This book is dedicated to my wife, Joyce, and our children, Nancy, Debra, Jimmy, Melissa, and Jamie, for all of your love and support for me in ministry, the sacrifice of going with me to minister to all people in different nations, cultures, and languages, and all the prayers you have voiced up to God for me in writing this book.

And, to our dear friends in ministry, the late Rev. Dr. Frank O. Hockenhull and to his widow, Dr. Marian Hockenhull. Rev. Hockenhull, you are truly missed and will always remain in our hearts. Thank you for your love for God and for your generosity to all people you have encountered in ministry. We love you. Rest in Peace!

CONTENTS

PREFACE

THIS BOOK HAS been brewing in my heart and mind for eighteen years. Arriving in the United States, I never thought there would be a segregation of worship. After ministering to the Maasai people, who truly were enemies of my tribe, I came to know that nothing is impossible with God. The adventure of prayer began in my heart as to how one day God would put all churches together in worship to Him. This developed more desire in my heart to start working on this ministry project.

My experience in working with different people of all walks of life, cultures, and languages made it even more desirable. I know God is able to abolish the segregation of worship and pull together His people to honor and glorify Him in love and harmony in His church. I wrote this book with pastors on my mind and with my heart in prayer for them. These shepherds of the flock are given an opportunity to lead God's church. When they lead by example and show the members of the church to open the door of God's church to anyone who visits, we will see all people of God worshipping together regardless of the color of their skin.

Not only were the pastors in my heart as I wrote the book, but Christians around the globe were also. In almost every church, there is segregation of worship, and this truly grieves God. I hope pastors, seminary professors, seminary students, Bible college students, church members, all Christians, and all people will find this book useful.

There will be no segregation in heaven. All born-again Christians will reside in heaven for all eternity. Let the people of God work out their petty differences and allow God to build His church here on earth without segregation. Southerners, Westerners, Easterners, and Northerners are all children of God and one family in Jesus' name. Let us do it God's way and not our way, and God will be glorified.

ACKNOWLEDGMENTS

I WANT TO acknowledge the servants of God who have truly played a big role in this book. They have prayed for the manuscript since day one and have encouraged me in different ways that led to the completion of this book.

Thank you, Stephen Wolfhope and Deborah Wolfhope, for your prayers, encouragement, and the great excitement you expressed in supporting me to write and publish this book.

Thank you, Dr. Stephen Rummage, for teaching me how to prepare expository sermons at Southeastern Baptist Theological Seminary and encouraging me to stand on my call to proclaim the message of diversifying God's churches.

Thank you, Dr. Joseph Perkins, president of Apex School of Theology, for your leadership and for bringing me in as a faculty member to continue your God-given vision to train church leaders for the twenty-first century.

Thank you to all of my fellow faculty colleagues at Apex School of Theology for your warm friendship and encouragement.

Thank you to all of my students at Apex School of Theology for your determination to learn and all of the prayers you have voiced for me and my family.

Thank you to all of my great professors at American Baptist College, Southeastern Baptist Theological Seminary, Trinity Theological Seminary, and the University of Phoenix for sharing with me such an inspiring treasure of academics.

Thank you Jonathan Levin for all of the prayers, encouragement, and support in this book project.

Thank you Debra Maingi for all of the typing you have done to make this book a dream come true.

Thank you Melissa Maingi for all of the typing you have done to make this book a dream come true.

Thank you, my wife, for praying for me and supporting me when time was very tight and stressful.

Thank you Forestville Baptist Church for all of your prayers and support and your love for God.

Thank you Johnny Brodie and Debra Brodie for all of the prayers and support in this book project.

Thank you Curtis Powell for all of the prayers and support in this book project.

Thank you Rosa Miller for all of the prayers and support in this book project.

Thank you Shirley Knight for all of the prayers and support in this book project.

Thank you Rev. John Bateman, Susan Bateman, Dominique Bateman, and Nathaniel Bateman for all of the prayers, encouragement, and support in this book project.

Thank you Eva Nash for all of the prayers and support in this book project.

Thank you Lee Bryant for all of the prayers and support in this book project.

ACKNOWLEDGMENTS

Thank you Glenn Frazier for all of the prayers and support in this book project.

Thank you Christine St. Jacques, my book project manager, and also the book editing department at WinePress Publishing, for your hard work in capturing the main thesis of my book and making it a dream come true.

INTRODUCTION

WHEN I WAS a teenager, I used to hang out with the son of a British man who was my dad's boss. One day we were horseback riding with our fathers when the young man asked his father, "Dad, why can't you change the color of my skin to look like Nicholas's?"

The father replied, "Son, there is nothing I can do to change the skin of your color to look like Nicholas's, because God is the one who created you like that, and him as well."

The young man replied, "Dad, I think it is true because the way I was last year is the same way I am today and my friend as well. But Dad, the way my heart was last week when my puppy was run over by a speeding driver is not the way it is today. My heart was heavy and very sad, but today I am happy and can sense the change of my heart."

The father replied, "Son, God has made your heart with room to change from sadness to happiness, and that is why you were sad last week and today you are happy."

This short story reminds us that God created us with different colors of skin, but that He gave us hearts that can change.

Every Sunday morning at 11:30 A.M. every pastor is in the pulpit ready to deliver the inspired Word of God that can bring change in the lives of the members. The hearts that gather every Sunday in the church come with spiritual expectations. The shepherd introduces his sermon with one desire in his heart: to see the hearts of the people changed forever.

That's why this book will tell us how we can allow God to change our hearts and listen to His call to abolish segregation in the churches. It will show us how to change hearts and abolish division in every church. Every Christian should see the urgency of answering that call because we are the ones who know what God is teaching us.

Every day we shop together in the malls, dine together in the restaurants, and attend the same schools together, but when it comes to Sunday morning, there is segregation of worship. The question remains, where in the world did segregation originate? This book will share with us and tell us where this great enemy originated. Then there will be some medication needed to treat this enemy. This book will give us the real dose to cure segregation in the churches. After receiving the dose, every Christian will have the joy of welcoming diversity in the churches. Then practical Christianity will become a great necessity in the churches, because the change of heart brings practical ministry in the hearts of Christians.

God has called His man as the shepherd of His flock. What is it like to have a real heart of a shepherd? This book will give us the answer to that big question. People of God, let us get ready to begin our adventure together as we all fasten our seatbelts and open our hearts to hear from the One who has all of the answers that we are looking for. This greatest teacher of all humanity is Jesus Christ. He has the power and knowledge to help us to abolish segregation in the churches.

CHAPTER 1 ∿

MEET THE AUTHOR: LEARN HIS TESTIMONY AND HIS CALL TO MINISTER TO THE MAASAI PEOPLE OF KENYA

ATTENDING AN EVANGELISTIC crusade in my home town in Kenya, I listened to the Word of God very closely. Being born in a non-Christian family, I never thought of any living God other than my ancestral gods. The truth of the Lord Jesus Christ as the only way, the truth, and the life was revealed to me for the first time in my life. The Holy Spirit was very much moving and speaking to me as the evangelist persisted in sharing the Word of God. Tears started flowing down my cheeks as I could not wait to accept Jesus Christ as my Lord and Savior.

The special moment in my life came when the evangelist gave the invitation to accept Jesus Christ as my personal Savior and I ran to him to show me how to become a child of God. I did it without fear or any shame. He prayed with me, and I received Jesus Christ as my personal Savior at the age of fourteen. That day I felt changed and went home excited and shared with my parents, brothers, and sisters.

Since that day, the Lord has given me the authority to go and take His Word to the lost people in the whole world. I have never regretted saying yes to Jesus Christ. He has been using me in His ministry in many different parts of the world to make a spiritual difference to many people from different backgrounds and origins.

The Maasai women worshipping God in music. These Christian Maasai women pour their hearts out to God in worship to Him. They are praising God (in Maasai Gospel Music) for the wonderful things He has done for them and their families.

My Call to the Ministry

As a native Kenyan, I crossed the enemy lines with the shield of faith, and God made my dream a reality. At the age of seventeen, I awoke in tears, confused from a recurring dream in which the Lord told me, a member of the Kamba tribe, to take the gospel to an enemy tribe in the neighboring Maasai region in Kenya. The Maasai people, who worshipped cows, had always been known as a primitive, savage enemy of the Kamba people. My mother and all of my family members warned me

2

that the Maasai warriors would cut me into pieces if I tried to share the gospel with them. But, despite repeated protests from my mother and grandmother, I could not dismiss God's call in my life. My biological parents were telling me I could not go, but I had to obey my spiritual Father.

Early in the morning, following the third dream in which God told me to take the gospel to the Maasai tribe, the enemy of my tribe since the beginning, I left home armed only with a small bag of clothes and a New Testament acquired from the evangelist who had led me to Christ three years earlier.

After walking more than seven miles, I approached the gate of a fenced-in village guarded by two warriors dressed for battle with spears, clubs, and long swords at their sides. I continued toward them until they stopped me with a hand signal. Despite the danger of the situation, I felt peace, because I knew God had called me there.

Suddenly, the warriors started charging toward me. I prayed, "God, it is now time. Take care of Your servant." The warriors abruptly stopped in their tracks, just twenty feet in front of me, and asked what I wanted.

I replied, "God, who created you and created me, gave me a message." In the Maasai culture they respect their so-called ancestral gods. They believe their god gave all the cattle in the whole world to them, but not to any other ethnic group. Hearing me mention God, they assumed that their god may have met with me. They led me in. The elders of the village assembled the villagers together. I gained acceptance from the tribe after drinking a tribal drink of a fresh cow's milk mixed with fresh cow's blood.

I presented the gospel of the Lord Jesus Christ to more than eighty people, and twenty-seven people accepted Christ as their Savior. For sure, they got the real message from the true and the only living God who is the creator of all humanity. I remained

3

in the village for the next three days, sharing the gospel while tribal messengers were sent to neighboring villages.

In this picture, the Maasai men, women, youth, and children are participating in the open air service crusade at a new church plant ground. They are participating in the service that Dr. Nicholas and Pastor Christian were Preaching. Usually, non-Christian Maasai men don't mingle with women and children in any formal gathering related to church worship. In this case, it is different; they are all in the same formal church gathering worshipping God. The power of God's Word in practical method is seen in this picture.

Over the next two weeks, several other villages came to hear me talk about Jesus. I even ventured into the deep jungle and led savage warriors there to Christ as well. Meanwhile, Joyce, my future wife, ever since her uncle led her to Christ when she was only thirteen, was praying to marry a pastor. The two of us met at a youth conference at her church. Afraid she would change her mind, I waited until after we were married to tell her of my ministry with the Maasai tribe. My wife exclaims to this very day that she was scared to death! Throughout her youth, the Maasai people had been at war with her village. She supported and followed me as her husband and thanked God for answering her prayer.

Joyce and I thank God for the ministry we had with the Maasai people. They are our friends, and we love and pray for them each day. Joyce and I ministered to the Maasai people throughout Kenya. As a result of our persistent prayers of reconciliation among these two tribes who had been great enemies since the beginning, and our efforts to proclaim the message of hope, love, and unity of the Lord Jesus Christ, the Kamba and the Maasai tribes are no longer enemies.

This picture is showing Mrs. Joyce (Nicholas's wife) and Mrs. Laura (Christian's wife) teaching Maasai women and girls. Their words are being translated by a Maasai woman from English to the Maasai language. They are teaching about the role of a Christian woman. The Maasai women are loyal to God and love their families.

5

Maasai History and Culture

The Maasai people are hard-hearted, failing to hear anyone who tries to convince them to leave and forget about what they know and believe. They are so culturally-minded that no one wants to change his or her mind and learn something other than his or her cultural trust. The Maasai do not believe in the living God, but they say that they know a god who gave herds of cattle to them, but not to any other tribe in the world. And this god, they believe, cannot be living, nor does he communicate with them.

The Maasai people have no idea of salvation because they say there is no living God and that the white people are the ones who lie that there is God and salvation. So they don't want to be lied to, and if they are lied to, whoever comes to convince them will be cut into pieces by their warriors with their long sharp swords.

The Maasai are a widely scattered but numerous Nilotic black people in East Equatorial Africa, whose habitat, down to the beginning of the nineteenth century, stretched from the Nandi plateau, the south end of Lake Baringo, and the southern slopes of Mount Kenya. In the east, the Maasai people were bounded by the Bantu and the Galla people of the region between the Tana and the Rufu Rivers.

The older name this distinct race of pastoral nomads adopted for themselves, or any other for the pastoral and warlike section of the original tribe, was "Ilmaa," which in the nineteenth century, if not before, became "IlMaasai."

The western and northern sections of the Maasai people, especially those sometimes known as "Iloigob," "Enjamus," or "Wasingishu," were not only cattle keepers and shepherds, but also industrious agriculturists. All sections of the Maasai people, agricultural as well as pastoral, speak basically the same language,

6

with variations resulting in two or three dialects. This language
is very similar to what the Lotuka people of the Mountain Nile
speak, as well as to the language of the Bari people of Southern
Egypt and Sudan.

This picture shows Pastor Christian teaching the Maasai men, being translated
by Pastor Richard. The Maasai men are very hard hearted to reach with the
gospel. They argue that church is for women and children, not for men. But
Pastor Christian taught them that God is for all people and God wants the
men to be spiritual leaders in their families. Some of these men shown in
this picture gave their lives to Jesus Christ and were baptized.

They are also related to the other members of the great
Nilotic speech group, the Nandi and the Kalenjin languages
of Kenya. The customs, and to some extent, the beliefs of the
Maasai similarly connect them with the tall blacks of the upper
Nile basin. Clearly, the progenitors of the Maasai emigrated
originally from the regions that now constitute the northern
provinces of Uganda. In all of their myths and stories, the Maasai

think of themselves as people indigenous to East Africa, and most of all to the regions around Mount Kenya.

This snow-crowned, lofty volcano of more than seventeen thousand feet in altitude plays a considerable part in their traditions and is supposed by them to be the habitation of a demi-god or goddess, Naiterukop. This god was said to be at the same time an Eve or Adam, the parents of the higher types of humanity. The Maasai population is approximately one-half million people.

The tribe of the Maasai had their own prophet by the name "Oloibon." He was there to bless the ceremonies of the *morans* (warriors) and to advise on propitious times for raiding and for war.

Loibons (plural) today deal with individual problems such as infertility and/or persistent misfortune. Loibons admit that they have general powers to foretell the future and still claim to be able to divine the causes of personal calamities.

Divination relies on a complicated method of counting pebbles thrown from a calabash. The Maasai also believe in a far-reaching divine power emanating from the sky high above the earth, and even above the lower regions of the atmosphere. This divinity, to which they can pray at times with real earnestness, is known usually by the female name "Enaai." Enaai is occasionally referred to as the black god, though in some minds there seems to be a triad consisting of Enaai, the greatest and remotest of all gods, and the god of the elements, the benign black god of rain. This god has interest in humanity.

Enaai and the black god, or both fused in one personality, would like to send rain to the parched lands below in perpetual abundance, so that there might always be fat pastures to feed the Maasai cattle.

In two days of open air service crusade, fifty five (55) Maasai people—men, women, and youth—gave their lives to Jesus Christ. This picture shows Dr. Nicholas and Pastor Christian baptizing the new converts at a nearby water tunnel, which is used by the Maasai people to quench their cattle's thirst. This baptism took place early in the morning, the first Sunday of the new church plant service. It was a dedication service for a new Maasai congregation called "*Oldoinyio Losiligi Baptist Church*" which means the "Hill of Hope." It was a new beginning for two Maasai groups that had been at war with each other for 20 years. The *Pruko Maasai* and the *Matapato Maasai*. God put an end to their war at this mission trip open air service crusade. For the first time in 20 years, people from both groups came together, prayed, and gave their lives to God, and they began a new chapter in their new lives in Jesus Christ as brothers and sisters in the Lord. The summer of 2010 became a great year for these two Maasai groups, which brought peace among them. It will remain in the history of these two groups as a turning point and a reconciliation year. Glory to God!

In one accord, the Maasai assert that no Holy Ghost exists because He cannot be seen, yet in another, they appear to believe that ghosts do exist and can only be seen by cattle, not by men.

As they do pray in their community, the Maasai have a very real belief in God, even if they are vague about his personality and uncertain whether they are praying to the great god of the firmament or to the black god of the upper clouds. The Maasai occasionally make sacrifices of sheep, a rite usually conducted by women, who as a matter of course pray twice a day, while men and children only occasionally utter prayers.

In these prayers, men and women associate the evening and morning stars and snow peaks of the great mountains, Kenya and Kilimanjaro, with the deity. They pray for children and for the health of their children, for rain, for successes in time of war, and plenty of cattle.

When one of their members gives birth to a child, the Maasai women gather and take milk, water, and firewood to the mother. They then slaughter a sheep, which is called a purifier of a hut or simply a purifier.

The women slaughter the animal by themselves and eat all of the meat, and no man may approach the spot where the animal is slaughtered. It is considered unlawful. When they finish their meal, they stand up and sing a song to the new mother and her newborn baby. Their song is as follows: "God to whom we pray, god who thunders and it rains, give me offspring. To thee only every day do I pray, thou who art of sweet savor like sage plants. To thee only do I pray, who are prayed to and who hearest. To thee only every day do I pray." Women and children also pray for rain.

The old men also pray in time of drought, charging round a bonfire of sweet-smelling wood into which is thrown a charm from the medicine man; their prayer is as follows: "Black god, Ho! God, water us, O, throughout the uttermost parts of the earth. Black god, Ho! God water us."

The young Maasai men pray that their battle raids may be successful and that they may bring back herds of cattle. All of these prayers seem to be differently addressed to god and the

10

morning and the evening star. Ceremonial events are directed
by a ritual expert called Oloibon (witch doctor), who, although
he has no political power, is the religious head of his tribe and
is very much respected.

Every adult Maasai man belongs to an age set. When he is
circumcised at the age of sixteen years, he joins the age grade
of *Ilmurran* (usually known as the *Moran* and often translated
as 'warriors'). After a period of seven to fourteen years, the
already—existing Morans are simultaneously promoted to
elders and are given a name of elderhood (*Iltekeyani*). In every
age set, the Maasai have a representative who plays the role of
consulting or solving matters of their religion and ceremonial
details, settling disputes, and taking care of administration. And
every age set also nominates, from among its own members, an
official known as *Olaiguenani* (chief), one who discusses who is
primus inter pares, or first among equals. He must be respected
for his wisdom and his diplomacy. Men's councils meet under
the shade of trees, and any kind man is said to give out shade
because people come to him for help and advice.

Although Olaiguenani is the chairman of the age-set council,
he is not allowed to make decisions without consulting his
age mates. After the initiation, the Morans graduating to be
Iltekeyani are expected to know about politics, religion, and
herd management. Moranhood forces the young men out
of the security of their homes to live in rough camps called
Manyattas, after which they return home as adult men, having
acquired the skills of social life and public debate needed for the
administration of the community. They also bring with them
a sense of superiority toward those who have not been through
the same experience, e.g., women, children, and outsiders.
Western education has been accepted gradually. By the 1950s
and 1960s, some Maasai boys went to primary school, hoping
later to become full-time Morans after circumcision.

Women are married at about the age of sixteen. When men are entering Moranhood, women too are circumcised. This is done shortly after the outset of physical maturity. The operation is regarded as parallel to male circumcision, for both mark the social transition into adulthood, and women do not marry until the ceremony is through. A man has to marry a woman from one of the five clans outside of his own. He is not allowed to marry the daughter of a man who is in his father's age set, nor can he marry two sisters of a woman belonging to his mother's immediate family.

When Moran males grow to manhood, start setting up a family, and keeping herds, they are allocated specific animals. On the wife's death, all unallocated animals go to her youngest son. When the husband dies, all unallocated animals go to his oldest son. The youngest son is automatically responsible for looking after his mother in her old age. The oldest son is responsible for his father. If any child were to abandon an aged parent, he would be cursed (cultural condemnation). The amount of formal bride wealth (dowry) traditionally requested by the father and brothers of the bride consists of perfect animals, five to ten head of cattle, and ten to twenty head of sheep and goats. The Maasai name for a cow is *en-kiteng* and after the gift—the dowry—has been made, the groom will be ready to take his new bride to his home.

Nine is a magic or perfect number for the Maasai, as it symbolizes the nine parts of the body. Nine of the cows are marked in color patterns, which are regarded as perfect, and therefore, holy.

The traditional Maasai diet is meat and cow milk mixed with cow blood. The Western world has also introduced the modern diet.

God has used us in a great way in Kenya and is continuing to use us as we minister in the gospel all over the world. We have seen many people saved and are still winning many lost people to the Lord, as well as ministering. The truth and fact is that in Philippians 4:13, Scripture tells us that, "I can do all things through Christ who strengthens me."

My prayer and desire is to see every living person throughout the world being reached with the gospel before Jesus Christ comes back.

My Philosophy of Ministry

My philosophy of ministry is based upon the teachings and examples of Jesus Christ as the Son of God and Good Shepherd who gave His life for the sheep. He has called me to win lost souls to the Kingdom of eternity, to lead His Church to the right channel and to the commitment of Jesus Christ, and by all means to lead His church to carry out the Great Commission that Christ gave to each one of us (Matt. 28:19–20). I also believe that the Bible's author is God, salvation is its end, and its matter is truth without any mixture of error.

My Call to the Promised Land

God called me to the promised land of America for His own great purpose. He called me here for a higher training for His ministry—which was not available in my native country of Kenya—as well as for ministry deployment in His mission field. All I knew about America was the history of this great nation and what I had learned in my high school geography class. But God's special call was for me to go to an unknown country according to my faith in God. It was another mission field like the one with the Maasai people. When the commander in chief gives an order to the troops to be deployed, no one should object. God, as my spiritual Commander in Chief, had assigned me the duty to be deployed to the promised land to proclaim His message of love, peace, and reconciliation.

This picture shows Dr. Nicholas preaching, being translated by Pastor Samuel who is a Maasai. He is translating the sermon from English to the Maasai language. A temporally structured pulpit is built on this church plant ground. This is in the middle of nowhere in the deep Maasai region where the gospel is really needed to rescue the Maasai people from perishing in sin.

In Harare, Zimbabwe, in Southern Africa, I participated in a pastors' ministry discussion at a Baptist World Alliance Conference. After driving for six days and nights to that conference, I led a team of forty-six men and women, following God's call in my life to advance His Kingdom. One day, I participated in the pastors' ministry discussions and performed music with the Maasai choir that accompanied me to the conference to worship and praise God in their Ilmaa language. Afterward, a very godly, loving servant of God, the Rev. Dr. Frank Hockenhull, and his wonderful wife Marian, at that time the pastor at First Trinity Missionary Baptist Church in the wonderful town of Flint, Michigan, came to me because God spoke to them both and revealed to them that something special, something

This picture shows Pastor Christian preaching, being translated by Pastor
Richard who is a Maasai. He is translating the sermon from English to the
Maasai language. A temporally structured pulpit is built on this church plant
ground. This is in the middle of nowhere in the deep Maasai region where
the gospel is really needed to rescue the Maasai people from perishing in sin.

"This picture shows Pastor Christian and his wife, Laura, along with Sarah
and Samantha, interacting with the Maasai people." They are having good
time with their new brothers and sisters in the Lord whom they had just
met within one week. Pastor Christian enjoyed drinking Kenyan hot tea.

This picture shows Dr. Nicholas left, Mrs. Laura, Miss Sarah, Matthew, and Pastor Christian at a pastor's conference. Pictured with them are diverse pastors from all Southern Baptist churches in the Maasai region. These pastors are Kambas, Maasais, Kikuyus, Kalenjins, etc., who have answered God's call to serve God in this part of the world. They come from different tribes, but have one purpose in heart: to abolish segregation in churches.

spiritual from God, was in me and needed to be enlightened. Dr. Hockenhull asked me whether we could go for lunch with him and his wife. I replied, "Sure!" Who would turn down such an invitation from a servant of God sent by God Himself to fulfill His mission?

During our lunch together, Dr. Hockenhull asked me where I had learned the Word of God, and if I were offered a scholarship to advance my training in the promised land of America, would I accept it?

I paused a little bit in disbelief, and my thoughts went back to my family and our ministry with the Maasai people. I looked at him and told him that if God provided a way for me, yes, I

This picture shows the church sign that was purchased by the mission team
for the newly born Maasai Congregation. From left to right, Mrs. Joyce
(Nicholas's wife), Sarah, Samantha, Pastor Dickson (who is the newly installed
pastor of the new church), Pastor Christian, and his wife Laura. Praise to God
for our home churches Bethany Baptist Church, Wendell, North Carolina,
and Forestville Baptist Church, Wake Forest, North Carolina—which enabled
the team financially to take the gospel to the Maasai people. And most of
all, thanks to my long-time friend Pastor Phillip Brantley, Senior Pastor at
Bethany Baptist, and his wife Peggy for their love for God, love for missions,
and desire to see every lost person on earth come to know Jesus Christ as
Lord and Savior.

will be willing to go the United States for higher education and
ministry.

The picture of that day at that lunch table still lingers in
my mind to this day. The next words of the man of God were,
"I will be praying for you, as you pray for us and see what God
will do on this." The exchange of contact information and the
last lunch together with the man of God and his wife, who were
strangers to me before I met them, was full of joy and praising

our God for leading us to meet and know each other in ministry. The hardest part of all was to say goodbye to my wonderful new friends who were ready to fly back to the United States, the promised land, that I had never seen and only dreamed of. Hugs and tears flowing down our cheeks were the only communication at that particular moment.

I didn't want to part with them because the friendship with my new fellow servants of God—Priscilla and Aquila from America—had grown so much within that one week we were together. It was the moment of truth and reality, because whether each of us liked it or not, we were to part from the land of Zimbabwe, but not in our Spirit of God in prayer. The only things about them that remained with me were the memories in my heart and mind and their ministry brochures. Whenever I thought of them, I would pull out their business card and hold it on my hands, hug it, and pray for them and my family.

The journey home for me and my forty-six men and women, which was to be six days of driving day and night, began. In my heart and mind I had this sweet information that I wanted to share with my family, but there was no way to communicate with them. Had I had access then to the technology that we have today—and for which I thank God—I could have called my family, in ministry with me, and shared the news of our good friends that God had given us.

Instead, I meditated on everything that was in my heart and praised God for everything that He had accomplished in Zimbabwe as many gave their lives to Jesus Christ during that week when the world saints of God met together to glorify the King of kings and the Lord of lords. We started praying for these two friends and their ministry. Prayer is a powerful tool; don't hesitate to use it all of the time.

When the couple arrived in the United States, sure enough they shared our experiences together in Africa with the First Trinity Church family. The congregation started praying for the family in Africa that their pastor and his wife had met. The next step was to find a way to get me the admissions information for the American Baptist College in Nashville, Tennessee, and for the college president to hear of a man in Africa who had something special spiritually that needed to be enlightened. Surely God was in the whole issue since the beginning, because the president told my friend Dr. Frank that he would be willing to give me a full scholarship to advance my ministry training. No one can change God's plans. He is never late, and His love is never limited by boundaries, distance, seas, or even oceans.

The admissions package had been put together and handed over to my friend to mail to me. Sure enough, the package was mailed from the United States, making its way to Africa. It surely made it to Africa fast, but it took three good months for me and my family to get it. Where was it? My personal opinion is that it was traveling in the whole Maasai region from south to north and east to west, because it arrived fine, but it had been passed on to many hands of young and old Maasai people that we had ministered to. To me, it was God giving them a message of consolation that He was calling Nicholas and his family away to minister to other people and that He would be with them.

All of this happened without our knowledge of any package arrived. It was not that the Maasai people did not want to give it to us, but it was far away from our house and was still on its way. There was no telephone for them to give us a call. The only UPS delivery was hand to hand until it came to my house after three months.

We prayed for the package, and we opened it, and it was the admissions information and a note from my friend. That was the beginning of our way to the promised land. We filled out the paperwork and mailed it to the college. Then we waited to hear from them. That did not take long or even go around for three months, but came straight to our post office in two weeks. All was good news of being accepted and being awarded a full scholarship. That was God preparing me and my family for a deployment to the promised land to minister to His people as we did to the Maasai people.

Then the preparations began for me to leave my family, our ministry with the Maasai people, church members, parents, in-laws, friends, and my native country of Kenya to the land of Nineveh where He had called me to minister to His people. And that Nineveh became the promised land of America. It was one of the hardest things in my life that I have ever experienced. Not being an emotional person, I kept it in my heart and to myself, and it was very tough, but God handled it for me and my family. The tough part was to say goodbye to my family at Jomo Kenyatta International Airport in Nairobi, Kenya.

The moment to face reality came when it was time to board the plane heading to the United States of America. The plane took off, and I said goodbye as well to the beautiful skies and tropical weather of Kenya. All that was in my mind was how I would reunite again with my family, and when. That was all that was in my mind, and thoughts were following each other every other minute. It did not take my seatmate long to realize that something was bothering me, and he asked me if I was okay. I replied no, I am not. He became worried and wanted to know whether there was anything that he could do to help me at the moment. I told him that for now, I really knew he couldn't help me, but my loving God would help me to go through it and I would be fine. He asked me again if I was religious. I told him yes, I was a pastor. He persisted on asking where I was going and what I would be doing there and was my family okay?

When he mentioned my family, sure enough he touched the wound and discovered the reason I was as I was when he realized that something was wrong with me. I told him I was going to the United States of America because my God had called me away from my country and away from my family to minister in His Word.

He looked at me and shook his head and said he understood how that would be painful to me because he and his wife had two grown children, and when they traveled, they missed them and their grandchildren. He said he and his wife were from Amsterdam in Holland and had been vacationing in Kenya for two weeks. Our conversation opened a door for me to start sharing the gospel with my friend and his wife.

He said, "Well, Pastor, we know there is God, but we don't see why we should believe in Him." I did not want to see the time pass away without explaining to those people how all the people in the whole world need God for eternal life. I shared the gospel with them on that flight, and even though they did not pray to ask the Lord into their lives, I planted the seed, and God's Word will never be void. I told them that the living God whom I just shared with them was the One sending me to America. Then they both said and acknowledged that pastors are good people. They wished me good luck as I went on and told me that they would be thinking about my family in Kenya and that we will be able to reunite again.

How I loved to hear those sweet words! It was encouraging and also God was telling me, "Nicholas, I have called you, and I have a plan for you and your family." The opportunity in the plane to share His Word with some people was a great confirmation. It was a long flight journey to Amsterdam, so my seatmates went ahead and took a nap, and I went back to my thoughts about my family and I continued to pray that God would reunite us again. The two days' journey to America was an experience that I will never forget because I told God everything that I knew about my family.

Arriving in the United States at Nashville International Airport was safe but different because it was close to winter. The only greeting I received was the very cold breeze that cut through my face when I was stepping outside the terminal to catch a taxi cab. I ran back inside because I had never experienced such a cold thing in my life. It reminded me of some very cold, fresh milk that had been refrigerated that my dad used to give me to drink when he worked for a dairy company.

Then, after stepping back to the terminal, I put my brains together and thought of the paperwork that had all the information from the college about America and the weather, and then I went back to my suitcase and got myself a jacket to help deal with the cold since I was used to only the year-round tropical climate of Kenya, East Africa. I put on my jacket and stepped outside and got a cab to the famous American Baptist College of the American Baptist Theological Seminary.

In twenty minutes, we arrived at the college. The view I was greeted by matched the description of the college my wife had been shown by God in a dream. It was a moment of another confirmation that God was saying, "I have decided to deploy you and your family here in Canaan to minister to my people."

God is amazing when He is involved in anything that He has started because no matter what the situation, He must accomplish His plans and purposes. As I unloaded the cab with the driver, some students noticed that a fresh man had arrived for college life. All were nice Christian men. And words from almost everyone were only three words: "Welcome to America."

My life was never the same again after I got into Griggs Hall, room 306. There in that same room was a bed and the clothes of another African student from South Africa who was not in the room at the moment.

After making myself at home in the promised land, I went on my knees at that moment and claimed, to God, that my family would come and reunite with me. I was very tired and sleepy because of the long trip. That kicked off my transition to America. It was a difficult transition because of the cultural differences. I never knew that there was a white church and a black church in America. All people in my native country—whites and blacks, yellows and blues—all worship together. That alone reminded me of the ministry with the Maasai people that God sent me to do in my previous ministry. It reminded me of Erankau Baptist Church where I was the pastor in the Maasai land and how God used my family and me to reach many other different ethnic groups that became part of our ministry with the Maasai. Then I remembered that in our church there were seven different ethnic groups. And I saw the reason why God called me to the promised land.

Every Christian should know the importance of worshipping together, because in heaven, all those who have accepted Jesus Christ as Lord and Savior will have no color. Heaven is for every believer who believes that Jesus is the only way, the truth, and the life (John 14:6). God expects all those who claim to be Christians to portray that truth wherever they are. I will talk about this in another chapter in this book.

When I arrived in America and found that black and white congregations worship separately, that alone made it so very difficult for me. I had not been told by the American missionaries that I served with for many years in my native country and Africa as a whole that there were black churches and white churches. I never thought that would ever happen, especially in America, the promised land. But it was certainly a reality.

I had to fast in prayer that the blacks and whites would come together in worship. In my first sermon in America, I preached about blacks and whites worshipping together in unity as brothers and sisters in Christ serving God. My family and I still pray that one day these churches in America will worship together regardless of the color of their skin, race, origin, nationality, or even gender. And God Himself who has started His good work in the lives of many saints in America will accomplish that at His own time (see Phil. 1:1–6).

We all eat together at the restaurants, so why not worship just like God intends—together? The best foundation of my theological background was set by my wonderful professors at the

23

American Baptist College. And in three years I was able to earn a Bachelor of Arts Degree and a Bachelor of Theology Degree. A wonderful group called the Silver Liners, from First Trinity Missionary Baptist Church in Flint, made their long journey to Nashville, Tennessee, to support me and my family in achieving what their pastor and his wife started—my acceptance at the college and receiving a full scholarship. These servants of God portrayed a very great picture of what it means to be dedicated servants of God. Even up to this very day they are a big, loving support for us in ministry and the entire First Trinity Church family. This is a true spiritual fruit from the true servants of God they have learned from and are still learning from—the Rev. Dr. Hockenhull and Mrs. Hockenhull.

After nine months of separation from my family, it was God's time for us to be reunited again. We all, as family and friends, had been praying for this reunion. It was a great reunion with my family after answering the call to His ministry in the promised land of America. God is never late, and at His own time He shows up when He is ready to fulfill what He has started. His plans never fail.

Finally, the family was together again for a sweet reunion and ready again as a whole to carry on the ministry that God had commissioned us to fulfill in the promised land. That will be addressed in another chapter of this book.

I hope you enjoyed meeting the author of this book and his testimony in the ministry and all that God has accomplished through him and his family in ministry among the Maasai people of Kenya. It is time to buckle up, saints of God, as I get ready to share with you the realities and the truths of abolishing segregation in the churches. Let the journey begin, and be ready to sail with me as we all learn together in this wonderful book what the Holy Spirit has put on my heart to share with you as we advance His kingdom.

Discussion Questions

- Do you know that your testimony can change someone's life?

- Is there someone you know who needs Jesus Christ in his or her life?

- Do you know God has a purpose in your life?

- If so, how would you fulfill His purpose?

- Have you answered God's call in your life?

- Do you believe that Jesus Christ has commissioned us to go to all nations to spread the good news?

- Do you know that your neighbor can be totally a nonbeliever?

- If so, what step have you taken to reach out to him or her?

CHAPTER 2

THIRTY MINUTES IN THE PULPIT TO CHANGE HEARTS FOREVER

SUNDAY MORNING AT 11:30 A.M. is a very important time of the Lord's Day in His church. The pastor steps up to the pulpit to deliver the message the Holy Spirit has given to him. That is the greatest moment of one's life, to proclaim the truth that comes from God, and Him alone, to His people. As the congregation pays attention to the man God has called as their shepherd, they long to hear what God has for them in that divine moment of truth.

People are looking for answers today because the world is full of violence and bad news every day. It is the responsibility of the man of God to bring the truth of God's Word to His children without any compromise. During the week, people are hurting inside. Some are struggling with different hardships of life, and others are facing sin in their lives and are looking for rescue. God has given the man of God the opportunity to help His children, but yet he gives them the wrong answer. As heavy hearts still wait for what can become the great news of their rescue, the pastor is supposed to bring to them the breath of God, which is His inspired Word. When the Word of God is compromised, the church is weakened, and God's people become spiritually anemic.

When you have bronchitis, you go to your physician, who will examine you and give you a prescription to go and get some antibiotics. When you get the medicine, you have to follow your physician's directions as you take your medicine. If you take it well, the cough will clear off, and you will get healed. But if you decide to not follow the directions, or maybe you add to your prescribed medicine some water to dilute it, it becomes useless and cannot bring healing for your bronchitis cough. In that case, you can keep coughing, maybe for the rest of your life.

That is what happens when we don't follow God's Word and what it has to say. If the pastor dilutes the Word of God, which is the real prescription He has given us, hearts will not be changed. The pastor is responsible for the spiritual well-being of the congregation. Their hearts are searching for real medicine that can change their hearts that are hateful, prideful, hard-hearted, segregative, etc.

The blood of the people of God is on the hands of the pastor. The great work of God in changing the hearts forever is the great work of preaching the Word of God truthfully. Preaching is the bringing of truth through personality, or the communication of truth, by man to men. The hearts of people cannot be changed with the power of a human being, but by the power of God's Word. The fruit of a change of heart is the love and unity that any changed person can have in his or her life. The world should see a great difference in the hearts of those who claim to be Christians.

The change of heart is something that every Christian should have in his or her heart. It will make such a big difference when we all learn how a change of heart would help to abolish division in every church. Spiritual change is what is needed in the hearts of people today. We should lead by example in whatever we do as Christians. But the question remains, how will they listen to the voice of God, who is able to convict them in His Word, when the preacher is not firm in his preaching of the Word of the Lord?

When the people of God receive the true Word of the Lord, it will convict them, and they will be totally spiritually changed. God loves His people, and He wants the best for them and their families. As the pastor steps up to the pulpit every Sunday, he should understand that he is preaching to people who have been saved and also those who have not yet been saved and are still searching for answers. He should not undermine them, judge them, dictate to them, or even force them. He should only love them, care for them, preach the truth of God's Word to them, and wait for the Lord to do His work.

The change of heart does not happen overnight, but it takes a time of prayer, patience, determination, and teaching. True change of heart happens in God's time. The pastor should not run out of patience when God is still at work, because God is never late, and His timing is always the best. The pastor is not the one bringing the change of heart, but God Himself is the One who is leading a person to make a decision in his or her heart.

A couple of years ago, I met one couple who had quit attending church services for many years. When I asked them why they had stopped going to church, their response was that in the church there is a lot of hypocrisy, and that alone is what has made them not go to the house of God to worship. I could see that this couple was in shock, having been driven away from church by Christians who could not walk, talk, and practice what they preached. I apologized to the couple for whatever may have happened and deeply encouraged them to understand that every person can commit sin, even the ones in church every Sunday. I had an opportunity to witness to them, and sure enough God spoke to them, and God changed their hearts from bitterness. They gave thanks to God, who gives mercy to His people and who gave them great joy and forgiveness. Today that couple has gone back to church and is very active in their Bible-believing church.

That is what we call a change of heart. What people are looking for in the church today is spiritual guidance and the right and true way to heaven. The pastor should not let the church of the living God be like a social club or bingo club or a cult where people meet to make each other feel good and be entertained instead of being taught how to obey God and how to live their lives according to the desires of the Lord.

God has given His people the Bible, which is the life manual that has all the instructions on how to live our lives. When someone is struggling with his or her life in a specific area, the Word of God has answers to that specific problem. That is why preaching the truth of the Word of God to the people without compromising it is the real answer to problems we are facing today.

Nine years ago, a young adult came to me and said, "I am so mad with my mother today and really want to move out of our house because I cannot get along with my mother. She does not understand that I have turned sixteen and am grown enough to make my decisions without her help. She needs to know now I am able to do things on my own, including everything that she doesn't want me to do."

I let the teenager get everything off her chest while my wife and I were listening, and when she stopped, I asked her if she was done.

Sure enough, she replied, "For now, yes."

Then I asked, "Can we help you now, whichever way we know how to, through the Word of God?"

The teenager said, "Yes, sir." By the way, she was a good Christian young lady. Then I told her turn with me to Exodus 20:12: "Honor your father and your mother, that your days may be long upon the land which the Lord your God is giving you." I let the young lady know that the fifth commandment, to honor one's parents, involves prizing them highly (Prov. 4:8), caring, showing affection for them (Rom. 12:10), and showing respect or fear, or revering them (Lev. 19:3).

She looked at me and said, "Are you telling me to change my mind and my plans to go back to that woman's house?"

I said, "Absolutely, yes, according to Scripture." We reminded her how her mom and dad loved her and cared for her, and they didn't want her make bad mistakes and choices that would hurt her life forever. My family and I knew her parents very well as servants of God who cared very much for their daughter. But the young lady was just having some teenager problems like any other. We helped her through that by showing her what God's Word said about that.

The young lady cooled down, and she understood that what her mother was trying to do was just to help her in her future life. She did go back home and made peace with her mother, and things went well for her.

Two years after that day, the young lady approached my family and me and said, "Thank you both very much for helping me when I was wrong and tried to disrespect my mother and decided to run away from home."

That is what happens when the truth of God's Word is taught or preached without compromise. It leads someone to change his or her heart forever. Today the young lady is grown. She pursued a nursing career and, I think, she is now a registered nurse making a difference.

God's Word has power to change hearts forever for the best. Every pastor who stands in the pulpit to deliver that powerful message should know that God's desire is for all people's hearts to be changed spiritually. The Word of God has to be preached truthfully to make one's heart change. The mistake we make in the pulpit today is when we dilute God's Word from solid truth to meaningless nothing. Hearts are beaten every day, twenty-four/seven. People are searching for something that can help their hurting souls and minds. The real Word of God preached conservatively will bring change in the hearts of the people of God. When the pastor fails to preach truthfully, the blood of God's people will be counted as on his hands.

I asked a pastor who was finishing his training in a conservative seminary how he would cope with the people that God would give him to minister to in his first pastorate if they were not be willing to follow the truth of God's Word. His answer was that he would probably preach the truth no matter what cost. That cost meant he would be ready to move on if the people refused to listen.

Each pastor should know that change does not happen overnight. Any pastor who is called by God in a liberal church should know that God has given him that golden opportunity to teach, preach conservatively, nurture, feed, tend, and mature His spiritually sick followers. The pastor should invest his time in that pulpit until God uses his preaching of the solid Word to change the hearts of the liberals He has given to him as his church members.

If the so-called conservative pastors are not willing to remain and preach in a liberal church, how shall we see changed hearts? The problem may not be the people, but the pastors. We have the Word, but are we choosing the kind of congregation we want to minister to? It is time for every conservative pastor to listen to the voice of God and allow Him to direct him to the needy people who need spiritual guidance conservatively. Nothing good comes without working hard to earn it.

Years ago, God called me to a small, very liberal Southern Baptist church that had history of changing pastors after every two to three months. That was the shortest time in the pastoral roster of that church. The pastor to stay the longest was there from 1859 to 1874—fifteen years of preaching. The next longest stayed for ten years, from 1986 to 1996. Then followed another one who stayed for three years, from 1997 to 2000, and I was his associate pastor. After that he was followed by another one who only stayed for eight months, and I was also his associate pastor. Then, after that one left, we began searching again for the next man to lead God's church as the senior pastor.

One day we called some candidates and started interviewing those who had submitted their résumés. After a couple of weeks of interviewing, one of the candidates, after finishing his interview, asked the pastoral search committee why they were searching for a pastor when God has already given one who had been their associate for five years. On that day, the committee pondered something they may never have thought about. The associate they had for five years had lots of experience in ministry, was very well-trained theologically, and had a heart for ministry.

Then a meeting was called for the church family to meet for a dinner and discuss the future of their church. The meeting was opened by prayer by the associate pastor, and after the dinner, discussion began. A lot of agendas were brought and discussed, and finally the pastoral-position agenda was brought up for discussion. It went around the tables a couple of times. The members were sharing their opinions on what kind of a pastor they would like to have. Very many good and bad requirements were voiced by the wondering flock that was searching for a leader. Then one member asked the church, "Why have we been looking for a pastor when God has given one as the associate who has invested five years in ministering to us even with and without the senior pastor?"

That was a moment of truth—for one of the most liberal churches that I have ever known—about to make a big decision for their church. The same person again persisted and mentioned my name as a proposal for the church to call me as their interim pastor. There were some "amens" in some parts of the dining hall and some silence in other parts. When God is ready to accomplish His plan, no one can stop Him.

The chairman of the deacons walked over to me and asked if I would be willing to be their interim pastor as they prayed and sought God's guidance. I told him that I had been waiting for the church to open their spiritual eyes since two years before that day.

But the silence that remained in one corner of the dining hall was where the heavy weight of the liberal chief was sitting. The reason was because I had made my stand in the beginning when I hadn't even been voted in as the associate pastor. They knew my stand on the Word of God. I can't compromise the Word of God.

That evening the decision was made for those who were present at the dinner to bring the proposal to the whole church for a vote. The whole church approved, 100 percent, to call me as their interim pastor. After a month, I received a phone call from one key leader of the church asking me if I would mind becoming their full-time pastor. I told the leader that I had been waiting for them to open their spiritual eyes for over two years. I finished by telling the leader, "God willing, I will be glad to take that position," knowing that there was nothing that I was to do that I was not doing before. It was just an adjusting of the position for the records. I had been performing the responsibilities of the pastor when there had been no senior pastor.

From that day, God began His work thoroughly in that church, which once had been liberal. As the pastor, I preached God's Word without any fear. I mentored the members, visited them as usual, and my wife, who is also a seminary-trained pastor's wife, continued to teach the women's Bible studies. The church members started to grow spiritually. Thirty minutes in the pulpit is a long time when the man of God is delivering the truth of God's Word without diluting it. Lives were changed in this church, and people began to make their stand in the Word of God. The Word of God stepped on their toes—and on mine as well. This church that was very well-known as a hard, dry, liberal church became one of the most conservative churches in the area.

Every pastor should know that when you invest your time in the church where God has called you to minister, lives will be changed. When those hearts are changed spiritually from the worst to the best, great things happen. That is why I am very much convinced that pastors have to make their stand in the pulpit and deliver God's Word without being afraid of being fired. Every individual who is employed in a certain company gives his or her best to do an excellent job; if not, he or she will lose the job. This, I believe with all my heart, applies more to the pastors to preach truthfully and conservatively the Word of God.

God has given us His Word to feed His people. When God is at work to change the lives of His people, no one can stop Him. The hearts of the people of God are searching for answers in their lives. The change of heart is a willingness of an individual who has been convicted by the Word of God. The responsibility of the pastor is to deliver the Word of God to bring the answers that the person has been searching for.

Earlier in this chapter I mentioned that change does not come overnight. What I meant is that people will hear and listen to the shepherd that God has given them, and with patience of the shepherd and the people of God, lives and hearts will be changed. Change of heart is not brought by the pastor but by God Himself through His living Word. It takes time to change something from how it is to the new way you want it to look like. In this case, patience is an investment of the Christian in his or her life.

When you are driving your car, you control the direction of where you want the car to take you. You don't let the car control you, otherwise, if you allow it to do that, you may enter into a big ditch. God's Word gives us directions for how we can have our hearts changed for the best, and we have to depend on God Himself to direct us. If you try to tell God what you want to do with your heart instead of allowing Him to help in bringing change in your heart, then it will be hard to experience a change of heart.

The Gospel according to John, in chapter 8, verses 31–32, says, "Then Jesus said to those Jews who believed Him, 'If you abide in My word, you are My disciples indeed. And you shall know the truth, and the truth shall make you free.'"

In other words, if you are truly a born-again Christian, you will have a teachable heart. God is asking us to have willing hearts that are ready to learn. When we learn the truth of God's Word about the change of heart, that truth will set us free. In the scripture above, Jesus was not as interested in finding capable people as He was in finding available people. Jesus was looking for teachable hearts. Each one of us, as His children, has to learn how to follow His directions so that we can experience the change of heart.

God loves all of His children, regardless of the color of their skin, their gender, nation of origin, ethnicity, etc. He wants each one of us to be humble and listen to His directions. Thirty minutes is a long time for someone who is willing to learn how to experience change of heart. We have to know that Jesus goes out of His way to prepare a heart to listen and learn. He waits for the moment we are most ready to obey. And while we can still refuse Him at any time, His rebuke is gentle. This woos me at the same time that it disarms me, making me willing and open and ready to change. If you haven't experienced the sweet aspect of our Savior's discipline, may I suggest that you spend a little more time in His Word and listen to His voice?

When one of your children develops a habit of disobedience, that will make you unhappy and very much concerned about what has really happened to your sweet child. Then you start searching for some answers about how you can help your child to be where he or she needs to be, the place before he or she had started swaying away. You invest time in praying and finding a better way to help your child. And true enough, a good parent will not quit until the child comes back in line again. That happens more to our God when we sway away, because we are His children, and when we don't want to follow His commands, He does His best to bring us in line. That is why He has given us pastors and His Word to learn how our hearts can be changed. The Word of God is truly powerful and capable of changing hearts forever.

Discussion Questions

- Do you feel any spiritual change in your heart?
- If you do, how do you respond to the new change of heart?
- Is your heart teachable?
- If it is, how can you help someone else to have a teachable heart like yours?
- Is there room for a change in your heart today?
- Is your heart searching for truthful facts about the Word of God?
- Are you willing to follow God's direction in your heart today?
- Is your desire to see someone's heart changed from sin?
- If so, how can you help this person who needs a change of heart?

CHAPTER 3

WHERE IN THE WORLD DID SEGREGATION ORIGINATE?

THE QUESTION OF where segregation originated lingers in the hearts and minds of many people today who are wondering about the existence of this great enemy that has attacked God's people for so many years. The answer to the question can be answered only by the Bible that God has given us as His guideline on how to live our lives and how to relate with other people whom He has created and put on this beautiful planet that He has given to us.

Without any doubt, we should truthfully know that segregation came from the Devil, who has always been on the opposition side to bring division and animosity among the people of God. When any person or people group allows this enemy to come between them, there comes a great segregation. I believe with all my heart that God's desire is for all of His people to live together and worship Him together in love and harmony, regardless of the color of their skin, their nation of origin, ethnicity, gender, etc. It is our responsibility as brothers and sisters in the Lord to work on abolishing segregation in the churches. Through prayer, studying God's Word, and fellowshipping together as we serve

Him, we can begin the mission of putting the army of the Lord together as we fight to abolish this monster we call segregation that has brought so much division among us.

In *Spectacular Magazine,* February 2008, my late friend and former colleague and professor at Apex School of Theology in Durham, North Carolina, the Rev. Dr. Archie Logan, Jr, EdD, published the article, "Enlightening, Empowering and Entertaining African Americans." It appeared on the religion page under the subheading, "Another Perspective: The Challenge of the Faith-Community." A longtime pastor, Dr. Logan wrote:

> As we enter 2008, African-American History month, the "Black Church" faces a critical challenge in Kingdom building and Christian witness. It is sad and difficult to admit, but "the church" continues to be the most segregated institution on the planet. It is estimated that over 90 percent of American churches remain segregated.
>
> The Bible says that all the races on the planet descended from Adam and Eve. In the book of Genesis, we read, "Adam named his wife Eve, because she would become the mother of all the living" (Genesis 3:20 NIV). In the New Testament, Luke writes in Acts 17:26, "He has made from one blood every nation of men to dwell on all the face of the earth."

Logan tells a story to make his point clear and understandable. As a young student at Wake Forest University in Winston-Salem, North Carolina, he learned in his anthropology class that there is only one skin color: a brown pigment called melanin.

> All people who have ever lived on the planet have the same skin color, just different amounts of melanin. For example, if you have very dark skin, it is because your skin makes a lot of melanin. Albinos have no melanin, so they have very plain or bland skin. Caucasians have only a little melanin; their skin is white. Brown skin comes from all the variations

you can get between white and black. Asians, Chinese, and Japanese have slightly thicker skin; the melanin makes the color a yellowish shade. No matter what skin color you have, it all comes from melanin. The melanin protects the body from the sun's harmful ultraviolet rays. Persons living near the equator have darker skin. Persons living in the extreme north and south near the polar caps have white skin.

As we move closer and closer to a total blended global society and culture, the church must seek to eliminate separateness and segregation. The age of technology has made worldwide communication and information-sharing almost instantaneous. Events are reported worldwide within moments of happening. In reality, the planet has become one large community and because we control our living environments globally, melanin has blended. Yet, most of us worship with those who look like us, think like us, and share common cultural worship experiences. Religion has become more sacred than the kingdom of God. It is time for inclusion and diversity in the faith-community.

Logan wants to start at home. As a member and pastor of an African-American congregation, he understands that both institutions—the African-American church and the Caucasian church—are segregated.

The roots of our faith-walk and religion have taken different directions. Although the religions of the world claim common values, morals, belief systems, and absolute truths, we carry out our mission and purpose in segregated faith-communities. The challenge of this millennium and postmodern age is to evangelize and receive into our congregations all persons without regard to culture, class, race, color, national origin, or economic condition. This is extremely difficult.

In most churches, issues of power and control override the Word of God. We are territorial; our churches are havens of comfort and false security. Many churches seek to do missions and kingdom-building but return Sunday after Sunday to the confines of their congregations, parishes, temples, worship centers, and synagogues. These are the places of protection and separation. As you experience Lent each year, meditate on a beloved community of inclusion and diversity: Heaven will not be segregated. (A. Logan, Ed.D, Executive Vice President, Apex School of Theology, Durham, North Carolina, 2008).

In addition to what Logan has just stated, today's church is under the attack of the Enemy, who has carried this weapon of segregation for a long time. It is time for every Christian man, woman, boy, and girl to stand together as a body of believers and abolish this monster called segregation. It can be done by all of the Bible-believing community saints, standing together as brothers and sisters in the Lord and carrying on the ministry of redemption, relationships, restoration, and reconciliation. Nothing is impossible when we do it according to the leadership of the Holy Spirit.

When God called me to take the gospel to the enemy tribe of my people in Kenya, East Africa, He helped me to understand the importance of putting the power of His message in the hearts of His children. Even though the animosity between my Kamba tribe and the Maasai tribe had been going on for many centuries, God had a way to abolish that animosity.

These two tribes never wanted to see each other eye to eye because of their cultural beliefs, upbringing, economic status, civilization, etc., and that caused so many years of going against each other and killing one another through war after war and flock smuggling. That happened until God touched my heart and called me to take the story of God's love, hope, and faith to the Maasai people.

Even though God knew they were the enemy of my tribe, He paved a path for me to introduce His Son, Jesus Christ, to them. He was the only One they had never heard about and the only

One who gave them the herd of cattle. That was the moment of truth and the end of the animosity that this monster, called segregation, had brought between these two ethnic groups. God was at work to accomplish what He had planned for these two people groups. He had to use a teenage boy from the Kamba tribe to take the gospel to his enemy. When God is at work, no one can stop Him.

The Maasai people accepted me through the power of God in their lives. I gave them the message of redemption, relationships, restoration, and reconciliation. God spoke to them, and He abolished the segregation and animosity that had torn apart these two groups for centuries.

Today, the Maasai people and the Kamba people are all together in ministry and many other different events and development of their region because God tore down that wall of separation. They worship together, serve God together, and they have extended their godly love and togetherness to many other different people groups. They made me their loving son and Joyce their loving daughter up to this very day. We love the Maasai people as our brothers and sisters and thank the Lord for the opportunity He gave to us and how He used us to give them hope for eternity.

What God did for the Maasai people and the Kamba people, He can do for other people groups. In Galatians 3:26–29, the apostle Paul reminds every Christian that through faith in Christ, all who believe become sons and daughters of God. This scripture is essential to every believer who has been called by God. Christians should emphasize the importance of abolishing segregation in the churches. Paul makes it clear to all people of God that when we give our lives to Jesus Christ, we become His sons and daughters.

What a brother and sister both do is share all things in love and embrace each other. There is a closeness in those two that no one can separate. The biological blood is thicker than water.

The spiritual blood of Jesus Christ that He shed on the cross to abolish segregation in the churches is thicker than any liquid substance.

The Bible speaks primarily to the church, but it also speaks through the church to the whole world. It is truly claimed by the Lord that the church can best speak to the world by becoming the church that is made by the Word of God.

When the church makes her stand on the issue of abolishing segregation, there will be a great spiritual movement to the whole world to bury this monster that has segregated God's people for so long.

It is known that some people who favor segregation appeal to the Bible in an attempt to justify their position. It is noted that in 1958, the book, *Segregation and the Bible,* by Methodist writer Everett Tilson, was used as a source. Some Bible scholars are translating the Word of God according to their opinions and not understanding the real meaning of Scripture. This kind of mistranslation has become a big problem and misleads people of God. It has brought much confusion in the churches.

This is a spiritual disease that is causing so much damage in the churches. The first person who is supposed to show others how to abolish this monster is the spiritual leader. There is nowhere else the people of God can hear the best method to abolish this enemy than to hear it from the pulpit—not just saying it, but truthfully translating Scripture.

I conducted a survey looking for some answers as to why segregation still exists in the churches in the twenty-first century. Some people said, "Because there is much hypocrisy in churches," "Because we have been raised segregated," "Because we are from the South," "Because of different worship styles," "Because of different cultures," "Because of not understanding each other," "Because we can only fit in our look-alike people group," "Because of the kind of music," etc.

These kinds of excuses have become the common sin that is committed by all people in churches today. When the people of God listen to His voice, they will welcome anyone who makes a visit to their house of worship. He or she will not be looked upon as though he or she has lost his or her mind by attending a certain church. God's presence is in every church that truthfully honors Him by allowing His Word to play a big role in the lives of the worshippers regardless of the color of their skin.

In this book, I talked briefly about the kind of people group God called me to minister to. As I stated, the Maasai people were enemies of my tribe. The Kamba people could not stand the Maasai people who claimed to own all of the herds of cattle in the world. Even though my ancestors truly believed the fact that the Maasai people were their enemies, God had some special plan of ministry in one of their own Kamba boys. Neither of the two groups could stop God from fulfilling His plan. God truly abolished segregation between these two people groups. God used me in a very tremendous way in proclaiming His Word to these very fierce, courageous people.

With their long swords, spears, clubs (*orinka*, as they call it in their Ilmaa language), and their well-decorated shields, God molded them and so they opened their hearts and found Jesus Christ, who changed their lives for the best.

The Maasai people have become one of the best friends of the Kamba people, and have, since knowing Jesus Christ, started intermarrying. Today, they are all brothers and sisters in the Lord and servants of King Jesus. Their sons and daughters have filled homes of both tribes, and children and grandchildren of both tribes have been born to them. There is no longer the animosity that existed for many years, but eternal love of Jesus Christ, which has dominated the homes and the churches in both areas. What has happened to these two tribes can happen to any people group around the world. All people are God's creation and should worship, serve, and advance God's kingdom together. There is joy and harmony in the church where the love of God and the emphasis of our Lord and Savior is honored and proclaimed.

Recently, my family and I visited a certain church in Wilmington, North Carolina. When we arrived at the church, we were welcomed by a man and his wife who saw us pull into the church parking lot. We truly looked different because of the color of our skin. But we were shown Christ-like love by the brothers and sisters in the Lord at that church. The couple told the pastor about us, and he came to meet us. He even introduced us to the congregation. We felt encouraged and saw the Lord's power at work in that church.

After the service, some people came to say hello to us. One elderly couple came to talk to us, and the man hugged me and pulled out a huge golden ring with the Christian cross on it and gave it to me. With tears on his cheeks, he said, "We are so glad you came to visit our church today. You are my brother and sister in the Lord." He finished by telling us to remember them and their church in our prayers and that they will continue to open their doors for many people who come to visit, regardless of the color of their skin.

It is time for each person who claims to be born-again to be color-blind and let God's church be the place where everyone can feel free and comfortable to worship. We are cutting off our own God's blessing when we allow petty and lame excuses of the past to interfere with our love for God and desire to serve Him together.

Every individual believer must understand the importance of going to the Bible to find the answer for how to abolish segregation in the churches. God is the One who has called His people to serve and worship Him in harmony. He emphasizes the importance of the gathering together of His church and giving Him honor and glory as we wait for His return.

In his book, *The Churches and the Social Conscience,* Olin T. Binkley, the first President of Southeastern Baptist Theological Seminary in Wake Forest, North Carolina, says, "The problem of race relations is a religious problem." He continues to say, "There can be no solution of the problem apart from religion; and religion is a powerful social force ... The churches in the Southern regions of the United States tried to protect slavery by the sanction of religion ... While Southern churches sought to justify slavery, the Christian impulse kept alive in many church members a respect for persons of both races and a desire to minister to human need and to relieve human suffering. Some members of the churches took an interest in the spiritual welfare of the slaves and provided religious instruction for them" (Binkley, 1948, p.3).

This tells me that every Christian should know the authority of the Scripture God has given to us and agree to have a fellowship of brothers and sisters in the Lord as we serve and worship. There are those who probably doubt whether God's Word has authority over us. It is quite clear that unless God gives us direction and answers to our problems through His Word, none of us can accomplish anything in life and ministry.

In this case, I believe that if every Christian in every church will rise up to abolish segregation in the churches, there will be the harmony of worshipping together. The message of togetherness in service and worship to God should not just be left to pastors alone, but to all Christians. We must understand the urgency at hand and step up to show the world how we can make a spiritual difference in this manner. Many of us do evangelism in our churches, probably every month. It would be a good idea to reach out to those who don't necessarily look like us. True Christ-like evangelism had been converted to a look-alike evangelism that focuses only on those who belong to a certain group color. Evangelism should be used to reach out to every lost individual, whether black, yellow, blue, white, rich, or poor. Jesus commanded us to go and make disciples of all nations. He did not tell us to reach out only to those who look like us, but to all people.

When God called me to the church where I am today, I told the church members that I believe in reaching out to all people with the gospel, regardless of the color of their skin. I started reaching out and won different people to the Lord. These are people of all colors and have become more involved in telling others about Jesus Christ.

The gospel of Jesus Christ is for all humanity. My church members have grown tremendously in their walk with God, and they respect each other as they all worship and serve God together. They pray for one another and love each other as brothers and sisters in the Lord. They don't really look alike, but they know and believe that God loves them all equally. Is it because they are more important than any other persons in the community? Absolutely not, but they know by the grace of God they are saved and should show God's love to others and should welcome them to church to worship and serve God together. The power to abolish segregation in churches will take each Christian to step up and face the Devil, head on, who brings this monster in our churches. The Devil works twenty-four seven while working on bringing the spirit of segregation in our hearts. We must understand that it is only those of us who claim to be born-again Christians who can lead by example and put our faith to work. We have to let our faith work for us as we take down this monster we call segregation.

I believe that the spirit of segregation begins in the human heart. If each one of us will be sold out for Jesus Christ, we will not have to welcome this sinful act of segregation in our lives and in the churches.

Ten years ago, I was invited to preach in a church by a friend of mine who is a pastor. This man of God went to seminary with me, and we took most of our pastoral classes together. He heard me share my faith and my theological stand regarding God's Word. He said to me one day, "Brother Nicholas, when God blesses me with a church, I would love to have you come to preach for us."

I told him that if it was God's will, that would happen. After one year, God gave him a church. He kept his promise and called me and asked if I would come to preach for him. I truly told him, "It will be my pleasure to do so." When my family and I arrived at his church, which was about an hour and a half away, we were welcomed by the pastor and his family. The worship service began, and we all started singing and worshipping. The preaching time came as always, and the pastor introduced me in the pulpit to deliver the morning sermon for the congregation. Halfway through the sermon, I started seeing some tears in different people's eyes. People were teary, and their cheeks were soaked with tears until the sermon was done, and some beyond that.

In my heart was this question: *Am I offending these people with what I am saying, or is the Word of God convicting these people?* As I persisted in preaching, I felt the power of the Holy Spirit whispering to me and saying, "Nicholas, don't give the Devil any chance to stop you from delivering the truth of God's Word to these people, because they need it." That became a moment of confirmation from the almighty God saying, "No matter what, preach My Word without any fear [see 2 Tim. 4:1–4]. You are my messenger, and the message belongs to me and must be preached with the power of truth."

I carried the message through to the end, and after I finished, the pastor came and stood with me at the front for an altar call. The pastor started inviting people to come, and the people responded tremendously. Some were still in tears, and others were holding their emotions strongly. The holy of holies was packed with many people who prayed to the living God for forgiveness, and others gave their lives to Him.

After the service, the pastor and I stood outside the door to shake the congregation's hands as they were exiting the sanctuary. Some people thanked me for the sermon, and others were upset with me that I had brought that kind of a sermon to them. One man shook my hand and told me that he never knew he would ever listen to a black man preaching to him. And now that his pastor had brought me into their church to preach, he would make sure the pastor was fired.

I told the man, "God brought me into His church to preach to you and not the pastor, because the pastor is only a shepherd of the flock, but the head of the church is Jesus Christ" (see Eph. 5:23). The man finished the conversation by telling me that he had been in that church for many years, since he was a little boy, and this pastor would have no pulpit next week to bring people like me to preach to them.

This story is just one among many stories that one would hear from different people in many different churches. When we let the Devil bring the evilness of segregation into churches, he will do it and destroy the harmony and true worship and togetherness of giving service to our living God and creator of all humanity.

It is the responsibility of born-again Christians to stand together and preach against segregation in the churches. One must understand that the pastor is called by God to serve Him; he is not hired by the church. The call for pastorship is a call from heaven but never a call from members of the church. One must never hassle with God for calling His true and faithful man to tend His flock. All born-again Christians must understand that we are soldiers in the army of the Lord and must stand together to defeat the Enemy within us.

Every member of every church around the world should stand by the Word of God and welcome the plan of abolishing segregation in the churches. We should never be hypocrites

50

who would say they love the Lord with all their hearts, but yet promote segregation in the churches. How will God forgive us of this kind of sin if we don't repent of it? Practicing segregation anywhere in the world, either inside or outside the church, is sin. Anyone who commits sin will be punished by God for violating His true and living Word.

There is no small and big sin; all is sin. God will never overlook one sin for another. Neither will God compromise His decision to punish anyone who commits the sin of segregation. If homosexuality (Lev. 20:13), fornication, and murder are sin before God, then segregation is also sin. Christians must lead by example and condemn all sins, not just some. The power of the Word of God will help us repent of these kinds of sins and make them right with God. None of these sins, nor many others that have not been mentioned, will be acceptable in the kingdom of God.

Let the people of God pull together as one team—"God's team in action"—to serve Him and worship Him in advancing His kingdom together regardless of the color of their skin. This will be God's answer to solve the dilemma.

Discussion Questions

- Do you know that segregation is sin before God?
- If you believe so, what steps have you taken to abolish it?
- Do you believe Christians should open the doors of their churches to everyone?
- If you believe so, what steps have you taken to make sure the doors of your church are open for all people to attend services?
- What would you do to help someone in your church who doesn't believe segregation is sin before God?

- Do you believe segregation comes from the Devil?
- If you believe so, what method will you use to stop the Devil?
- Do you know segregation weakens God's church?
- Are you willing to welcome someone of another race into your church services?

CHAPTER 4 ～⃝

THE REAL DOSE TO ABOLISH SEGREGATION IN CHURCHES

WHEN I WAS at Southeastern Baptist Theological Seminary in Wake Forest, North Carolina, as a student, I remember Billy Graham's grandson sharing with me a story of his mission trip to my native country of Kenya. He told me how he was so very blessed to arrive in Africa to share his faith with Kenyans. He told me how he saw many people who were thirsty for the true Word of God. He and the whole team that went with him were so thrilled to lead many people to Jesus Christ. He finished his story by telling me how much the whole world needs evangelists today, including the United States of America.

I totally agreed with him that every human being on the globe needs Jesus Christ as his or her personal Savior. And the only way to do so is to provide the Word of God to all people groups on earth. Do you know that the real dose to abolish segregation in churches is doing evangelism to all people groups of the world? The world we live in today is full of people who are perishing in sin. Unless we take the gospel of the Lord Jesus Christ to them, they will still continue to perish in their own sins.

In Matthew 28:19–20, Jesus Christ commanded all Christians to "Go therefore and make disciples of all the nations, baptizing them in the name of the Father and the Son and the Holy Spirit, teaching them to observe all that I commanded you; and lo, I am with you always, even to the end of the age." Jesus Christ has given us principles and patterns of evangelism in His New Testament church, and New Testament churches recognize Jesus as the Lord. So, any program of evangelism they follow must take into account the pattern He Himself designed. This kind of pattern is not mechanical, but spiritual. One should term this as Evangelism in the Ministry of Jesus Christ.

As it is written in John 17:11, Jesus Christ addressed God as *Holy Father*. This suggests not only the moral character of God, but His exalted nature as well (see Isa. 6:1–3). Jesus Christ, in His evangelism, considers the four qualities that can make one succeed in this kind of ministry as He provides the real dose to abolish segregation in churches. These four qualities are holiness, righteousness, truth, and love. In the Bible, God's righteousness is presented as mandatory, as seen in the Ten Commandments. All of these are associated both with Jesus' reference to the character of God and with His own redemptive ministry.

Herschel H. Hobbs, in his book, *New Testament Evangelism*, says, "Though Jesus was the Son of God, even God Himself never regarded deity other than in an attitude of supreme reverence Man has a corrupt nature which must be changed (Matthew 23:25–28). So, regardless of man's position or personal attainments, Jesus Christ said of him, 'Unless one is born again, he cannot see the kingdom of God' (John 3:3). Jesus Christ never taught reformation, but regeneration" (Hobbs, 1960, p. 64). He regarded man as of infinite worth (Mark 8:36).

Though man is lost from God (Luke 15), his salvation is so worthy an enterprise as to call for God's mightiest work to seek and save him (Luke 19:10). So, this attitude should posses every child of God. The Bible does not say that some have sinned and come short of the glory of God, but that all have done so. Outside of Christ, the junior child is lost. The cultured lady is lost. The wealthy banker is lost, and the scholar is also lost. So, evangelism must center its mission of rescue in the community of palatial mansions as one receives the real dose to abolish segregation in churches.

Jesus Christ used preaching, teaching, and healing as methods in His ministry. Following His temptation experience, He came into Galilee, preaching the gospel of the kingdom of God (Mark 1:14). Then later, after He went into Capernaum and immediately on the Sabbath day, He entered into the synagogue and taught. He also healed many.

Hobbs says in his book that Jesus came to save man in his entirety. Whether in preaching, teaching, or healing, His approach was directed toward revealing Himself as the power of God unto salvation. Every phase of Christian work should be to that end. If it cannot so justify itself, it has no place in the program of a Christian, a church, or a denomination. A teacher should visit and teach for a verdict. The healing ministry of Christian hospitals should be but a means to an end. God's healing powers can heal a body and soul.

Jesus placed His major emphasis upon teaching. To Him, teaching was not merely the recitation of facts. He taught people, but not things. Teaching is designed to instruct the mind, while preaching is intended to move the will to action based upon the things taught. Jesus did both of these things in His teaching. He instructed the mind and challenged the will. He varied the method of His teaching. Sometimes it was by precept, and at other times by example. His methods might be in parables, through nature study, or by questions and answers. He often used the project method of teaching. At times, He taught on the basis of events of the moment. Jesus found truth in His Scripture. He was not a slave to any one method.

In His teaching, Jesus ran the entire gamut of human need and emotion. Anyone who aspires to teach for Him should study His methods, content, and purpose. An examination of modern methods of teaching reveals that Jesus used all of them. After two thousand years, man, by mental development through trial and error, has only approximated in part that which was inherent in Jesus' methods of instruction. Jesus also seeks for the lost. Of Himself, He said, "For the Son of Man is come to seek and save that which was lost" (Luke 19:10).

Lost souls also seek for Jesus to heal their souls. People like Andrew and John left John the Baptist to seek Jesus (John 1:35). Nicodemus sought Jesus by night and found the light of life (John 3:1–12). In His dying moments, a thief sought Jesus, and arm in arm, walked with Him through the gates of glory (Luke 23:42–43). Even Jesus Himself did not end His soul-winning effort with those who came seeking Him or who were brought to Him. He came to seek and to save those who were lost. Early in His ministry, this truth is affirmed.

Jesus also sought the lost through His followers. On two different occasions, Jesus sent them forth on definite evangelistic missions (the twelve, Mark 6:7; the seventy, Luke 10:1). In the case of the seventy, it is specifically stated that He sent them before His face into every city and place where He Himself would come (Luke 10:1). Like John the Baptist, they were to be forerunners preparing the way for Him. No person who aspires to be a soul winner can wait for others, either to come or to be brought to Him. If he would follow the example of Jesus, he must be actively engaged in seeking the lost.

The real dose to abolish segregation in churches would require evangelism in the life of the New Testament church. When God completed His redemptive work through His Son, He entrusted the proclamation of it to Jesus's disciples rather than to the angels. Other than Jesus, only sinners saved by grace can preach and teach properly the gospel of grace. The effectiveness of that preaching and teaching is by the power of God.

God would reveal the understanding of His Word to His people as they proclaim the real meaningful dose to abolish segregation in churches. In Jesus Christ, the first-century Christians found the full and final revelation of God. These first-century Christians accepted the lordship of Jesus Christ.

On the day of Pentecost, Peter declared, "Therefore let all the house of Israel know assuredly that God has made this Jesus, whom you crucified, both Lord and Christ" (Acts 2:36; see also 1 Cor. 2:8). The early Christians confessed Jesus as Lord (Rom. 10:9). They prayed to Him as Lord (Acts 7:59–60). They wrote in His name (1 Cor. 7:10). Their abilities were recognized as gifts from Him (1 Cor. 12). The church experienced the presence of the Lord (2 Tim. 4:17). Jesus is and was the Lord of the church (Eph. 5:29). To the church, Jesus was the blessed and only potentate, the King of kings, and the Lord of lords (1 Tim. 6:15).

The first century Evangelism can be also understood in the twenty-first century effectively, which still provides the real dose in abolishing segregation in Churches. In no case did the early Christians compromise this belief for the sake of outward uniformity (1 Cor. 12:3–6). The early church had a planned ministry. This is seen in Acts 6 where the church set apart seven men to assist the apostles in God's ministry in His church. The Word of God increased, and the number of disciples multiplied in Jerusalem greatly and a great company of the priests were obedient to the faith (Acts 6:7).

It is quite important for the believer to obey the guidance and leadership of the Holy Spirit. The early Christians knew the Holy Spirit as the divine agent in evangelism. In response to Jesus' admonition, they waited for the Holy Spirit's power. In his book, Hobbs says that at Pentecost, this power was manifested not only in outward appearance, but also in the preaching of the gospel, and in the saving of three thousand souls (Acts 2:1–4). In danger, they found assurance in this power (Acts 4:31). By Him doors were opened, not only jail doors (Acts 5:19), but also the doors to men's hearts (Acts 8:36) and of entire nations (Acts 13:2). Everything that is done or written was by the power of the Holy Spirit. The Holy Spirit is God. Indeed, He guides men in their serving and desires to dwell in them.

If the techniques seem to stifle the Spirit, it is the fault of the performers and not the fault of the planner. Furthermore, churches may well cooperate with one another in evangelism as they all strive together to provide the real dose to abolish segregation in churches and other worthy causes. The increasing results of simultaneous evangelistic crusades attest this truth. New Testament Christians are independent people, but they express their independence through willing, volunteer cooperation.

When Scripture speaks, God speaks, and all Christians must listen to what God says about evangelism. It is quite important to know that the evangelizing, preaching, or teaching one does in churches, homes, schools, and even in the community must begin with God.

Scripture states, "But you shall receive power when the Holy Spirit has come upon you; and you shall be witnesses to Me in Jerusalem, and in all Judea and Samaria, and to the end of the earth" (Acts 1:8). That statement was Christ's last message to His disciples. He told them that unless they had the power of the Holy Spirit granted to them, they could not witness for Him. The Holy Spirit is the only One who can grant that power, that privilege to go out and be a witness for Him. Without the Holy Spirit's power, all people's work for Him is in vain.

In his book, *When God Moves in Revival,* Festo Kivengere makes this powerful statement: "Revival begins at the cross." Kivengere suggests the fact that He (Jesus Christ) carried our sins and sicknesses. He was wounded for our transgressions, bruised for our iniquities, and the punishment that should have fallen on us fell on Him instead. He accepted the consequences of our rebellion. Because of our selfishness, Jesus went to the cross. By piercing Jesus—allowing blood to drip down from His body, this body being torn from all of the beatings He took—the whole world was saved. That is what God wants all people to share with the rest of the world—the good news, the gospel of Jesus Christ.

Charles S. Duthie asked in his book, *God in His World,* "How can one know God?" The simplest response he gave as the answer is, "Through Jesus Christ, our Lord. As an evangelist, one must seek to explore and understand whether his faith is strong enough to help others make great discovery of what salvation means to one's life. Evangelism is not about what man wants to share, but what God wants us to share. In all one does and shares, God must be the heart of it all."

In the words of Newman R. McLarry, "If God is a cosmic force, and thus impersonal, He cannot know personal man. Therefore, the very thing a group contends, and is defeated—they limit God." That is to say, if one tries to do missions without knowing God, then he has no business out there trying to evangelize. It was only through Jesus Christ, the Son, and God, the Father, and through His evangelical teaching, living, atoning, and thinking for people's sins when He came to this world as an evangelist, that people have access to the Holy Bible. So, for one to be an evangelist, evangelism itself must start with God.

One can very well connect this point with the previous one because everyone has learned that evangelism starts with God, and that only He can grant anyone the divine power to go and evangelize the unsaved souls in this world. Since it is God's prerogative to tell everyone evangelists, what message one should send out to reach the lost souls, it makes it one's duty and mission to tell the world "thus says the Lord." Evangelists can accomplish this mission by doing some essential things that make anyone an effective evangelist for Christ. One must have one's heart clean of all filthiness and lathered with holiness and willingness to do God's Will. One must pray and ask the Lord for salvation and commit oneself to do His will. Also, one must pray for one's wants and needs, in light of one's missionary work, and must be sincere.

Stanley Brown says, "Every Christian teacher should think of himself as an evangelist." That first word in quotation marks, *every,* means *all.* Therefore, everyone can be an evangelist for Christ. All that one should do is be prayerful and the Lord will give one leadership and guidance on His mission. God did not send just preachers to evangelize, but He also sent apostles, prophets, evangelists, pastors, and teachers to better equip disciples for mission and for the edifying of the body of Christ (Eph. 4:11–12). James Robinson says, "As Christian leaders, one should obtain a knowledge of His Word in order to accomplish His Will and to be fruitful in His Service."

A certain church in Kenya has four strong Bible study departments that can educate Christian leaders to reach the world more effectively with the Word of God to win souls to Christ. These four departments are Sunday school, Wednesday night Bible study, Bible drill team and Bible study, and vacation Bible school. The Sunday school is an institute of teaching and learning that involves class studies, lesson reviews, and hymn singing. The program opens up with a hymn—primarily one that fits the lesson each Sunday—a word of prayer, a devotional reading, and breaking off into classes to teach the Bible to young people so they may become better witnesses for Christ. All four of these departments involve making disciples. It is a part of the Great Commission. However, these are just a few of many ways one can win souls to Christ.

Carl F. H. Henry says that God's Word makes demands upon us. And with each demand there come the dynamics to enable everyone to obey. There are three passages of Scripture that would each stand for one demand. God gives everyone three demands, each involving Christian mission. These three demands are found in Matthew 5:16; 28:18–20; and Mark 16:15. These demands have one thing in common, the Great Commission. In those three passages, Jesus tells everyone to go and deliver the Good News to this hungry world.

With respect to Matthew 5:16; 28:18–20; and Mark 16:15, one would make these three demands relate to the wise who kept their lamps trimmed and burning. The unwise did a foolish thing. They went on their mission with their lamps but had no light, because they had no oil. Now those who were wise had light in their lamps, because they had oil. So the foolish asked the smart folk for some oil, but the people were reluctant to give it to them. They needed the oil because their lamps burned out. But the wise still refused. It was their way of teaching the unwise responsibility for priorities (Matt. 25:1–9).

In addition to the lamps they had, they were also given some talents to use until the Lord rewarded them. So, they used them and began to multiply those talents the Lord gave them by making more talents. The Lord saw that they were very productive in their many talents and blessed them and rewarded them by saying, "Well done, good and faithful servant; you were faithful over a few things, I will make you ruler over many things. Enter into the joy of your lord" (Matt. 25:21).

Today, Christian leaders ought to do the same (following this example in Matt. 25:1–9, 15–17, and 20–21) by being independent leaders and keeping their lamps trimmed and burning, and being responsible and not depending on others to do their work when they have the capability to do it themselves. Above all, they must use their evangelistic talents, as evangelists for Christ, to train their church congregations for world mission. And by doing that, six things will be fulfilled: reaching persons for discipleship training; orienting new church members; equipping church members for discipleship and personal ministry; teaching Christian theology and the Baptist doctrine, Christian ethics, Christian history, church policy and organization;

training church leaders for ministry; and interacting with and undergirding the work of the church and denomination.

As evangelists, leading the congregation into world mission simply by using all of the six evangelistic methods given by Roy T. Edgemon, is doing the work of discipleship training and will provide the real dose to abolish segregation in churches.

The first part of this chapter dealt with God giving the evangelist the message He wants the evangelist to share with the world—obviously, the gospel of Christ. This part will connect to the next when the evangelist takes the message, the gospel of Christ that God gave to His disciples, and truly uses it to instruct congregations, the disciples, to go out into the world and bring the lost souls to Christ that they may be saved. It is very important to know that any disciple—an evangelist who is guided and taught by God and the leadership, and who receives strength from the Lord—can go into the world, into every nation, to win souls to Christ. This is the Great Commission being put into practice. There are two groups of disciples that I would like to address.

The first group is comprised of the disciples who are made and instructed by the evangelist to go out and preach the gospel to every person. And the second group of disciples is made up of the souls who are being won to Christ by the first group of disciples. The first group of disciples wins the second group, the group of lost souls, to Christ. This is called discipleship.

And what is discipleship? There are at least two meanings of the term. One meaning is given by David R. Currie: "It is the continuing daily process of responding to the call to follow Christ." Christ gives us the other definition: "When He had called the people to Himself, with His disciples also, He said to them, 'Whoever desires to come after Me, let him deny himself, and take up his cross, and follow Me'" (Mark 8:34).

But the main question is, which of the two is the true meaning of discipleship? The answer is: both. For did not Jesus, in Mark 3:14, appoint "twelve, that they might be with Him and that He might send them out to preach"? And did He not say in Mark 16:15 to "Go into all the world and preach the gospel to every creature"?

Now one should notice that neither of those verses sets time limits on the preaching. But common sense can tell that if we are to feed every hungry soul in this world with the bread of life, then it would take days to fulfill this mission—better yet, our whole life! The mission is nonstop until the day of judgment, the day of Jesus' return, after the names are called up yonder.

But it is not sufficient simply to say that discipleship is a continuous process of sharing Jesus' gospel with the whole world. For discipleship is a "square mission." Discipleship is making a commitment. God made the covenant with the Israelites that His law would be placed in their minds and their hearts (Heb. 8:10). So, God makes a commitment to the people as Christian evangelists. He commits to work in us as we believe in Him (Phil. 1:6). If He can lay a commitment on His people's hearts, a message from heaven, then it is their beholden duty to commit themselves to win souls to Christ by telling them the Word of eternity that is providing the real dose to abolish segregation in churches.

While discipleship is making a commitment, one must also commit to teach God's Word. The prophet Isaiah taught the Word of God. He made a commitment to teach the multitude "to prepare the way of the LORD, making His paths straight. Every valley shall be filled, and every mountain and hill brought low; the crooked places shall be made straight and the rough ways smooth; and all flesh shall see the salvation of God" (Luke 3:4–6).

David Currie says that, overall, He taught the people to

clean up the acts of this world by winning souls to Christ. And to do the job of such kind, one must have the proper attitude,

63

for it is true that attitude is the key to being a true disciple. One must approach lost souls positively, not negatively. And if we as evangelists approach people with that kind of attitude, they will follow us likewise. Thus discipleship is teachable. But, discipleship doesn't stop there. Discipleship is having a relationship with someone who does not know Jesus Christ as personal Savior and leading the person to Jesus. We were made for meaningful relationships.

We were created to share life with God. Evangelists must have a relationship with God by studying His Word so that they can relate to those whom they win to Christ.

In completing the square mission, one must be mindful that discipleship is a responsibility. "Christianity involves grace and responsibility," Currie says. "Anyone's responsibility of bearing a cross and being God's partner in ministering to the world results from the calling."

Jesus entered into Capernaum. There, He met a centurion, a man whose servant was ill. The centurion asked Jesus to heal his servant with the divine Word of God. Jesus, having been forewarned of the servant's illness, a paralysis, responded to the servant's need and immediately took action (Matt. 8:5–8).

To sum it up, Jesus had a responsibility. His responsibility was to save a victim from becoming a statistic. He had to uplift him with power from heaven in order to keep him away from death and back into the swing of things in life. So then, with that in mind, our responsibility, as disciples of Christ, is to save a dying, sick world from becoming a victim of death from sin. We have to give Christ the same souls God has given to us, the same way He gave them to us; only in that way will they be renewed in the Spirit everlasting.

While we, as evangelical disciples, are on our soul-saving or soul-winning adventure, we may run into a lost soul who will ask the question, "What must I do to be saved?" When we are faced with that question, we must give them a "square answer." A square has four sides.

On the first side of the square, we answer the question by saying, "Before you can be saved, you have to realize that you are a sinner." We can reasonably refer back to the passage in Matthew 8:5–8 where Jesus heals a sick servant. We can picture in our minds, just by looking at verse 6, that the servant was so sick that he was conscious of his illness.

On the second side of the square, we can answer the question by saying, "Having realized that you are a sinner, the next step is that you have to have a desire to be saved." Looking again at verse 6 of Matthew 8, we can see through the servant's consciousness of his illness that he had a desire to be saved. That's why Jesus wanted to heal the suffering servant. Then, once the lost has established the fact that he is a sinner and is willing to be saved, then that person must pray in sorrow. This is called repenting of your sins.

On the third side of the square, you must repent of your sins to Jesus Christ and ask Him to forgive you. The fourth side of the square is that you accept Jesus as your personal Savior. These four sides of the square give us the total answer.

We, as Christian disciples, have a mission. Our mission is to go out into this world to win and save souls to Christ. And whenever a lost soul presses the question upon us, "What must I do to be saved?" then, we must tell them that, to be saved, you must realize that you are a sinner, must have a desire to be saved, must repent of your sins, and ask God for the gift of salvation. This point leads us from the disciples of Jesus Christ to the lost souls being won to Christ.

Paul, the apostle, as an evangelist, preached to King Agrippa. He told him all the things he had been through with the Jews and Gentiles. Paul told him to turn away from his evil ways and turn to God, repent of his sins and ask for forgiveness. Paul knew within himself that King Agrippa had a belief in him as a prophet, a disciple. Paul, himself, believed that he was a disciple of Christ. So, Paul won King Agrippa to Christ and really was committed as an evangelist of the Word of God and a soul winner. In this case, Paul provided a real dose to abolish segregation in churches.

When all Christians take their Great Commission calling seriously, they will be able to provide the much-needed Word of God that will lead sinners to repent of their sins and be born again in Christ. At this point, we know that lost people, who were once lost and now are found, live in a world with the lost who need help finding their way. Spiritual leaders and evangelists can help these kinds of people. God has put evangelists in the ministry to be well-equipped with flashlights that one might light up the dark pathways for the lost so that they may be able to see their way and be led to heaven. What is so great about the mission is that one can ask God for the perfect message to deliver to the disciples, and one can feel free to instruct the disciples, relating to the perfect model, who is Jesus, to go out and win the lost to Christ.

Following that kind of model, one has the evangelistic chain that can never break. The chain is so strong that the lost can be pulled into heaven without the fear of falling back down to the earthly sins again. One can accomplish this mission that can turn the world from the losing side to the winning side. And now that one has connected all five of these links, one has the perfect chain that must pass around to every lost soul in this world. Having a grip on this chain, the souls will be won to Christ, the mission will be accomplished, and the world will be a better place to live in.

Theologically, when all of this has been said and done, it will be evangelistic and the educational work will lead many to know how important it is to provide the real dose to abolish segregation in churches. The accomplishment of this kind of mission takes study, a desire to do God's will, prayer, and faith that God will lead, guide, and teach the way. As one journeys through and tries to help the lost out of these dark tunnels, the Holy Spirit, together with God, is with us in the picture.

This reflects the method of winning one-on-one evangelism, which can be practiced more in every church, neighborhood, and nation in the world. In this case, an evangelist, being led by the power of the Holy Spirit, can apply this kind of strategy and win many souls to Christ. Every born-again Christian is an evangelist who can do this ministry and bring people to Christ. This is because there is someone special, called the Holy Spirit, who is energizing, equipping, and working for Him.

After an evangelist decides to serve this only One with power, God gives him spiritual knowledge so that he can overcome any kind of evil spirit that tries to make the soul-winning ministry unsuccessful. Any spiritual improvement in evangelizing can be powerful if one puts effort into studying the Word of God, praying without ceasing, and then practicing what one has learned so that the fruit can be obtained.

Also, one who desires to be a strong evangelist, so as to win souls to Christ, should be a member of a church body where he can fellowship with other converted believers who will also give him courage to serve God faithfully and successfully. After being in a position of doing this, one has to follow God's will and guidance so as to win lost souls. Being an evangelist, one has to keep his spiritual lamp burning so as to be available at any time when a lost soul shows up. An important fact for anyone to know as an evangelist is that he should deny himself daily, take up the cross daily, and follow God in serving Him in His ministry. In regards to being God's faithful evangelist, one should understand that winning these lost souls is the key point of being a good, faithful disciple in the mission field and providing the real dose to abolish segregation in churches. To foster a close spiritual relationship with God, he must also relate to those who will be won to Christ.

One must be mindful that discipleship is a responsibility, and Christianity itself involves grace and responsibility. And the responsibility of bearing the cross and being God's partner in ministering to the world results from one's calling to ministry. Also, as a disciple of Christ, one has the responsibility of saving a lost, dying, sick world from becoming a victim of death by telling a lost person how to be saved, realizing that he is a sinner. The sinner should have a desire to be saved, repenting of his sins and asking God for forgiveness and for the gift of salvation.

Discussion Questions

- Do you have a heart for evangelism?

- If yes, how involved are you in doing evangelism in your church?

- Do you know someone in your community who is not a Christian?

- Is there a family member in your family who is not a Christian?

- If yes, how concerned are you for his or her life after death?

- What is your plan to make sure your relative is saved from sin so that if anything happens, he or she will be in heaven with you someday?

- Do you believe that Jesus Christ has commissioned us to evangelize?

- Do you believe that all Christians should reach out to all people and share with them the plan of salvation?

- If yes, are you willing to reach out in your community and tell someone of another race about Jesus Christ?

- Do you know that there are many people groups in the world that are still perishing in sin?

- If yes, what steps are you taking as a Christian to reach out to them and win their lost souls to Jesus Christ?

- Have you thought about taking an international mission trip to another country to share the Word of God?

- If yes, are you working on forming a partnership with a missionary who is working overseas to invite you to help in sharing the Word of God with the lost people in that country where the missionary is serving?

- Do you think God might be calling you into full-time ministry?

- If yes, have you shared with your pastor and the church about your new call to serve God?

- Are you familiar with the International Mission Board of the Southern Baptist Convention?

- Are you familiar with the North American Mission Board of the Southern Baptist Convention?

- Are you familiar with the National Baptist Convention, USA, Inc?

- If you answered yes to these questions, please contact these agencies for more information.

CHAPTER 5

THE JOY OF DIVERSITY IN CHURCHES

WHEN I WAS a student at American Baptist College in Nashville, Tennessee, I woke up very early in the morning one day to get ready for my first class. Then I looked through the window and I saw very beautiful blossoming flowers outside. Those flowers were different colors and very attractive. I decided to take my camera and walk down there to take some pictures. As I was walking, the thought came in my mind of how wonderful it is to see the beauty of God in His creation. These flowers were not planted by anyone, but God planted them naturally. He did not ask for any type of advice from any floral professional about what kind of floral colors He should come up with, but He decided to beautify His own earth with all His power.

I truly saw a glimpse of God's floral diversity with those flowers. Their beauty spoke for itself and led everyone at the college to talk about their attractiveness. It was the power of God portrayed in His own creation to all humanity.

This incident reminds us of how God has created all of the people on earth with different skin colors for a good reason. He decided to beautify His own creation with different handsome and beautiful people who are His children. In His plan, God wants all people to live together in harmony and promote the diversity He invented during His creation.

In the same manner, God wants born-again Christians to emphasize the importance of diversity in His church. If God has begun the plan of diversity in His creation, how can we undermine His decision? All people are God's creation and should be allowed to worship together as they serve the almighty God. God wants His people to be unified as they carry on His ministry. The divisions are being brought by the Enemy, who doesn't want to see the power and the authority of God prevail.

I personally believe that the beauty of God's diversity in His church should be emphasized by every person who claims to be a Christian. Today, churches are declining because we have decided to invite only those who look like us in our churches. When every believer in the church becomes color-blind, the diversity will be strong, and many people will be reached by the gospel, and the kingdom of heaven will be advanced. The joy of diversity will speak for itself, and many will be saved. We will be able to learn from each other, and the ministry of heaven will be stronger than ever.

Diversity in God's church can be achieved through inter-racial marriages, or integrating with African Americans, Latinos, Caucasians, Europeans, and/or other ethnic people groups, all in one congregation as God's church. It does not matter whether one is from Africa, Europe, America, Mexico, or any other nation in the world. What matters is the original diversity God planted on earth during His creation.

None of the people groups mentioned above should be seen as outcasts when God leads them to seek membership in any congregation. As long as the congregation is a Bible-believing church, one should be welcome to be part of God's church. One might ask, what would be God's reaction if anyone would deny one's becoming part of His church? Or what would God do if a leader from any of His people groups is disrespected because of the color of his skin?

Digging deep in the book of Numbers, we find that there is dissension between Aaron and Miriam and their brother Moses.

> Then Miriam and Aaron spoke against Moses because of the Ethiopian woman whom he had married; for he had married an Ethiopian woman. So they said, "Has the LORD indeed spoken only through Moses? Has He not spoken through us also?" And the LORD heard it. (Now the man Moses was very humble, more than all men who were on the face of the earth.)
>
> Suddenly the LORD said to Moses, Aaron, and Miriam, "Come out, you three, to the tabernacle of meeting!" So the three came out. Then the LORD came down in the pillar of cloud and stood in the door of the tabernacle, and called Aaron and Miriam. And they both went forward. Then He said,
>
> "Hear now My words: If there is a prophet among you, I, the LORD, make Myself known to him in a vision; I speak to him in a dream. Not so with My servant Moses; He is faithful in all My house. I speak with him face to face, even plainly, and not in dark sayings; and he sees the form of the LORD. Why then were you not afraid to speak against My servant Moses?"
>
> So the anger of the LORD was aroused against them, and He departed. And when the cloud departed from above the tabernacle, suddenly Miriam became leprous, as white as snow. Then Aaron turned toward Miriam, and there she was, a leper. So Aaron said to Moses, "Oh, my lord! Please do not lay this sin on us, in which we have done foolishly and in which we have sinned. Please do not let her be as one dead, whose flesh is half consumed when he comes out of his mother's womb!"
>
> So Moses cried out to the LORD, saying, "Please heal her, O God, I pray!"

Then the LORD said to Moses, "If her father had but spit in her face, would she not be shamed seven days? Let her be shut out of the camp seven days, and afterward she may be received again." So Miriam was shut out of the camp seven days, and the people did not journey till Miriam was brought in again. And afterward the people moved from Hazeroth and camped in the Wilderness of Paran.

—Numbers 12:1–16

The Word of God has revealed to us that Moses was a very faithful servant of God. He was loyal to God and had a good, close relationship with Him. The servant of God had married an Ethiopian wife, and it looks like dissension arose between Moses and his siblings because of this marriage. If one has a doubt why this should not be viewed as an interracial marriage problem, which Miriam and Aaron did not approve for their brother Moses, then one should ask why God was not happy with them. And especially Miriam. To my understanding, it seems as though this is a resentment of race against race. If this episode had pleased God, He would have not have allowed the leprous disease to attack Miriam. God had been disappointed by the way these siblings treated their brother due to his marriage to a woman from another race.

Should we today not take caution from what happened to Miriam and let God do His work, as He is the source of marriage? What God has begun, no one should interfere with. Why would God lead His faithful servant Moses to choose an Ethiopian wife if she was not provided to him by God Himself? Why would God make Moses a leader of His people if it was sinful to get married to a woman outside his race?

Many of us today want to do things our way instead of God's way. I believe each one of us must follow God's way, because it is the only way that can lead us to the promised land. There will be diversity in God's church when every person represented in God's church remains loyal to God's plan of diversity. The

74

bickering that has crippled God's church for many centuries because of our selfish motives and hypocrisy has truly hurt God's ministry. The only better way and strategy to allow God's will to be done in His church in the twenty-first century is to die to self and live for Jesus Christ. He will help us to look at things beyond the color of our skin.

Numbers 12:10 reveals that the wrath of God showed on Miriam's body immediately. It did not take long to show her that it was wrong to bring dissension because of her brother's decision to accept the will of God in marrying an Ethiopian woman. Should this kind of lesson learned by Miriam open our eyes to know that when God speaks, we must listen and obey? According to my understanding of Scripture, when Scripture speaks, God speaks.

None of us should question God as to why He designed marriage to be between one man and one woman. God did not say that if you are a black man you should get married only to a black woman, or a white man should marry only a white woman. God chooses your companion for you when you believe in Him and obey His leadership. We tend to dictate to our living God whom we should marry or not marry. No one should stop two people whom God has put together for marriage, as one man and one woman for a biblical marriage.

A couple of months ago, there was a news item about a beautiful, white young lady who had fallen in love with a handsome young black man. Both of these people were good Christians who had attended church together for a while and were both born-again Christians. They were members in a church where some of the people did not approve of their relationship because of the color of their skin. When they requested to use the church facility for their wedding ceremony, there was a debate as to why they should be allowed to use the facility when one was white and the other was black.

To my understanding, church leadership called for a church business meeting to vote for whether to allow the young couple to be married in the facility or not. The ballot was cast, and the small majority said, no, these two, both God's people, could not use the facility for their wedding. I believe there was a split in this church after that vote.

Is this how God wants His people to live their lives as hypocrites and segregators in the name of Christianity? According to my spiritual experience, I believe this church missed some glimpses of God's glory after they cast their vote to deny the couple to be married in the sanctuary where they had worshipped for years.

Maybe this story represents many other Christians and churches out there who cannot understand how a white woman could fall in love with a black man or a black woman could fall in love with a white man. They are all beautiful in God's creation. Why should we become a stumbling block to their marriage? When God gave Adam a good, deep sleep to make him a suitable companion, He did not say that He was to make a different companion geared to the color of his skin. I think we have allowed a spiritual disease to affect our lives miserably by denying diversity its role as God designed it in His Holy Word.

Moses had a great love for his siblings and truly cared for his sister Miriam and his brother Aaron. After his sister Miriam had been affected by the leprosy, Moses cried to God in prayer for his sister's healing. Aaron's repentance of his sin toward his brother Moses due to his wife led to God's intervention and answering Moses' prayer of healing for his sister.

I believe we all as Christians need to repent due to the committed sin of segregation that has crippled God's ministry for many years. We should turn back to God and lead His church to move toward reconciliation and move on to bring more diversity in His loving church. When God looks down on earth, what kind of Christians does He see in us? Do we represent Him in a humble, honorable manner, or do we grieve Him for the way we conduct ourselves?

Earlier in this book, you read about the author, born to a Kamba tribe in his native country of Kenya. The fact of the story about the Maasai people and the Kamba people is that they could not see eye to eye with each other because of the animosity between these two tribes. But, when God penetrated deep into their lives, He changed their hearts, and they became brothers and sisters in the Lord. The animosity that existed for many years was no more. They stopped attacking each other and stopped killing each other. Instead, they became very close friends that led them to open up to intermarriage.

The Maasai sons and daughters started dating sons and daughters of the Kamba tribe. God took those who had been great enemies for many years and brought them together and made them sons- and daughters-in-law. The diversity in marriage that God invented in His Holy Book, the Bible, was put to work in a practical way. Instead of the Maasai people looking at the Kamba people as outcasts, God blessed them with beautiful children. God was honored and continues to be glorified for the tremendous work He has accomplished among those two people groups.

I personally ministered to the Maasai people, Kamba people, and many other people groups. They were all together, glad that God put them together as a team to advance God's kingdom. God blended them for one purpose and one mission, to represent His plan of creation. These people groups have won so many people groups to the Lord, and God's kingdom continues to grow each day. If they had not listened to the voice of God, they probably would still be stuck in their past ungodly beliefs of hate and segregation. The diversity they brought in their relationships and their churches has spoken volumes. They have learned each other's culture and language, and are all serving

God together in joy and thanksgiving. They bear each other's burdens and love each other as brothers and sisters in the Lord. They respect each other and support God's mission on earth as God-fearing people.

God wants His church diversified as His Word is diversified and has changed the lives of all people. The best strategy to abolish segregation in the churches is to let the power of diversity take root in our hearts and in the churches. Many people will be saved, and God will be glorified.

I want to give advice on how we can approach this issue of segregation that has crippled churches and families for so long. Being an expert in cross-cultural ministering, I can speak through experience about how we can help to heal these broken relationships. First of all, you should feel free to sit down and discuss the issues without any fear. When you bring up the issue and put it on the table for discussion, relax, pray together, and let one person lead the discussion. Ask each person from a different race or ethnic group to bring either one or two issues to talk about. Be open and truthful. You cannot allow fear to dominate your lives for all eternity. Ask questions like: Why is it that we blacks don't get along with whites? Why don't whites feel comfortable to interact with blacks, and vice versa? What can help blacks and whites to start fellowshipping together? What can we do to teach black kids and white kids, Latino kids, etc., to play together in our communities, schools, churches, etc.?

When these questions are brought up and discussed with openness, you will find solutions, slowly but surely. The old wounds, which had been created by the tension between these races, will start to heal. Things get out of hand because we don't want to discuss them and solve the differences. Every race group has some cultural beliefs and can teach others the uniqueness of its culture.

Christianity is a global belief, and each person must be willing to love like Jesus and minister like Him. When we put our differences aside and learn how to live with each other and how to worship together, there will be harmony, and the joy of diversity will be celebrated in the churches. This will be the beginning of a lifelong learning process of each other's culture. But, as Christians, we should be willing to know that the best culture is the culture of heaven, which Jesus Christ has written for us in His Holy Bible.

If the church can stand together in repairing the damage caused by segregation, everything else will fall into place. God has given the church the responsibility to teach His Word, which has the power to instruct His people about how to follow His teachings and guidelines. It is the churches that have let God down in this area of teaching. Second Timothy 3:16–17 says, "All Scripture is given by inspiration of God, and is profitable for doctrine, for reproof, for correction, for instruction in righteousness, that the man of God may be complete, thoroughly equipped for every good work."

In 2 Timothy 4:1–5, the apostle Paul tells us:

> I charge you therefore before God and the Lord Jesus Christ, who will judge the living and the dead at His appearing and His Kingdom: Preach the word! Be ready in season and out of season. Convince, rebuke, exhort, with all longsuffering and teaching. For the time will come when they will not endure sound doctrine, but according to their own desires, because they have itching ears, they will heap up for themselves teachers; and they will turn their ears away from the truth, and be turned aside to fables. But you be watchful in all things, endure afflictions, do the work of an evangelist, fulfill your ministry.

The church that stands for the Word of God and teaches it faithfully without compromising it will lead its members to love like Jesus and minister like Him. This kind of a church will not have a problem walking the walk and talking the talk as they abolish segregation in churches.

I have seen people in my church, who love each other as brothers and sisters in Christ, love like Jesus and minister like Him. These are Christians who have given their lives to Jesus Christ and don't have a problem interacting and worshiping with people of another race. They respect each other and embrace each other with godly love. They all share the good and tough moments together. They worship and serve God together in gladness. They bear each other's burdens. They are God's creation and servants who have denied themselves daily and have taken up the cross to follow Jesus Christ. They know this life here on earth is a temporal life, and they understand the requirements of going to heaven. They are color-blind Christians who only want others to know Jesus Christ as Lord and Savior. They want all people to worship and serve God together as one team.

The October 11, 2011, issue of Southeastern Baptist Theological Seminary's magazine, *Outlook,* notes that Dr. Daniel Akin, the president of this great institution in Wake Forest, North Carolina, preached a sermon at Binkley Chapel. He drew his message from Mark 11:12–25. Akin reminded his audience of Jesus' admonition against those who fail to be fruitful in ministry work. Akin went on to say that fruitlessness now may result in fruitlessness forever. He persisted to say, "Lose your usefulness for Jesus, and He may curse you and move on!"

He reminded those who attended the service that morning, including students, faculty, staff, and all guests, that it is not Jesus who needs us. Akin said, "As of this moment, the Southern Baptist Convention remains a mostly middle-class, mostly white network of mostly declining churches in the Southern United States of America." He went on to affirm, "Those are the undeniable facts, and must change or we will die." He also noted that the serious problem is seen not only in the Southern

States, but is pervasive in all Southern Baptist Churches across America.

Racial bigotry is explicit and implicit in most churches, especially in the Southern Baptist realm, Akin said. He gave sound advice to the Southern Baptist Convention and told them what they really need. He said that what we need is a heart change. Akin plainly stated that, as Southern Baptists, we need an inward transformation that will result in an outward transformation that will result in our churches on earth looking more like the church in heaven (*Outlook*, 2011, p. 28).

In support of what President Akin said, I want to say that I have been a Southern Baptist minister all my life. I have served in Africa and traveled all over the globe. I serve in the United States, and we truly need a denomination that is open to all people regardless of the color of their skin. If we want people of every race on earth to be reached by the gospel, we need to open the door of our denomination as well as the doors of our local Southern Baptist churches. We Baptists are Bible-believing people, and we should follow what the Holy Book says about the inclusion of all people in worship.

When we lead by example, God will bless our denomination, and we will see success in abolishing segregation in churches. Many people will come to know the Lord as their Savior. We cannot segregate ourselves and still claim to be Bible-believing people. Action speaks louder than words. Jesus did not choose a certain race group and favor them or minister to them alone. He reached out to all people, regardless of the color of their skin. This must be our motto as we strive to reach the world for Jesus Christ. No matter how much we talk about Him, if the door of our denomination is still not open to all people, we are being disobedient to God. As Southern Baptists, we address many areas that dishonor God and do our best to teach what the Bible says about those areas, from homosexuality to women as deacons in ministry. But when it comes to segregation, we remain silent!

What are we going to tell Jesus Christ when He comes and we are still segregated? Don't we understand that God knows our hearts and all that we do in weakening His church? I believe with all my heart that segregation is sin, just as homosexuality is sin. In many cases, when we don't act against this monster that has crippled God's churches for many years, we truly qualify as hypocritical.

As Southern Baptists, we have gone to almost the ends of the earth reaching out to the lost people groups with the Word of God. We truly have a great heart and desire to see every lost person on earth be saved. I believe with all of my heart that if we all can gather together in the oneness of the leadership of the Holy Spirit, we can abolish this monster we call segregation that has separated us from one another in worship to God. It can take only willing hearts and obedient people of God to defeat this enemy. There will be no other people who can take care of this enemy except those of us who claim to be born-again Christians. We must understand the power of unity and blessing with which God rewards His people when they obey Him.

When God created all of us, He did it because we mean so much to Him. He is our Father and Creator. The color of your skin doesn't matter. You are His child and should be loved, respected, ministered to, and treated as an equal. There can be great joy in the church when all Christians are united together in worship to God. Jesus Christ died on the cross for all people, regardless of the color of their skin.

I believe that all interracial couples should be allowed to worship in any church they choose to attend. In my church, all of our members have opened wide their hearts, hands, and the door of our church for all interracial couples to be part of our membership as we all serve God together and worship. I believe this should happen in every church on earth. These are God's creation, and should be loved, embraced, and welcomed in every congregation that meets to honor and glorify God. This kind of service to God will bring joy to all people as they embrace each other, and diversity will grow tremendously.

Discussion Questions

- Do you believe there should be more diversity in every church?

- If yes, what steps have you taken to make sure your church is diversified?

- Do you have a heart for a woman who is married to someone of another race to be supported and encouraged to attend the services in any Bible-believing church and not looked upon as an outcast?

- If you do, what steps have you taken to make sure every interracial married couple feels welcome in your church?

- Do you have a heart to minister to the children of interracial couples?

- If you do, what is your plan for reaching out to them with the gospel?

- Do you think your church will allow these interracial youth to mingle with other teenagers in your church?

- How will your church respond to a black or Latino youth dating a white girl or boy, or vice versa?

- Do you rejoice on the fact that heaven is a diversified home for all born-again Christians?

- If you do, what steps have you taken to make sure your church looks like heaven?

CHAPTER 6 ❧

PRACTICAL CHRISTIANITY AS A GREAT NECESSITY IN CHURCHES

MY WIFE IS a good cook. Every time she goes to her kitchen, she takes a pot or skillet and puts it on the stove, ready to cook whatever is on her menu for the day. I have watched her using pots and skillets to prepare all of the delicious meals I have eaten in my married life. I can testify that I have never seen or heard any pot or skillet tell my wife, "I don't want to be used today!" These wonderful cooking instruments are always ready to do their designated, practical work. If they complained that they were tired of burning and being used for cooking our meals, we would starve to death. Praise be to God that the pot and the skillet are committed cooking instruments for their work.

This illustration gives us an idea about what each one of us should do to commit ourselves to practical ministry in churches. When every member of the church is sold out for Jesus Christ, he or she will have the desire to serve God with commitment. Digging deep into Proverbs 16:3, we see it tells us to commit our work to the Lord, and our thoughts will be established. The word *commit* comes from the Greek word *ergazomai,* which means to work or to render service. In other words, each

Christian should commit himself or herself fully to work for the Master. God intends for every church believer to be committed to serving Him.

When a Christian pours out his or her heart to the master in commitment to rendering service to God, God approves the request and pours His blessing upon the Christian. The secret of God's blessing in service to Him by a Christian is one's willingness to serve the Master with gladness. Practical Christianity is a necessity in churches. The church cannot function without God-fearing members. These members should be willing to devote themselves fully to serve the Lord in His church.

The contribution of service to God by every member in the church makes it more fun for them and easier for the ministry. All believers attend church because they want God's blessing in their lives. None of us would say, "I don't need God's blessing." So, we must understand the responsibility that God has given to each one of us in service to Him. One cannot serve God by proxy, and nobody should give an excuse to not serve God. Individual commitment to God is a necessity in His church. The children in the church nursery need some willing, faithful Christians to take care of them as the parents attend worship services. The hailing family or person in the hospital needs a visit by the minister and also by the fellow members of the church. The struggling teenager needs the pastor/youth pastor and some other Christians to help him or her in the struggle. Aging senior citizens need all of our love and kind deeds in ministering to them in their golden-age years.

This kind of practical ministry is essential to the life of the church. We cannot overlook this kind of ministry, because people are hurting, and they are looking for spiritual guidance and support. Whether a struggling person is a member of the congregation or not, the church is responsible for reaching out to the person and helping. Christians are dependent on God for help as they serve Him in this capacity. God will be glorified, and His struggling people will receive the spiritual care they so desperately need.

When I was a student at American Baptist College in Nashville, Tennessee, I received a phone call from my wife, who was in Kenya at that time. She broke the bad, sad news to me that my sister had passed away. On the phone, there was shock and disbelief that my sister, with whom I had grown up and was very close, was no more. At the moment I needed some help to deal with the big loss of my dear sister. As my wife took the responsibility to minister to me on phone, I was terribly miserable about the sad news. The conversation was calm and soul-comforting at the moment. But when the conversation was over and my wife and I ended the phone call, my grieving period began. I had no family member in America at that time. It was the saddest moment in my life. I went to class, and when the professor was teaching, my mind was still dominated by the sad news of the loss of my sister. I could not take it anymore.

I picked up my book bag and headed back to the dorm at room 306 in Griggs Hall where my life in America had begun six months earlier. I went on my knees and prayed for myself, my family, and my sister's husband and children. After the prayer, I cried so hard inside the room and asked God for strength and comfort. There was no family member around me to share the grief with me. I decided to leave the room and just take a walk. I walked behind the dorm and decided to go to a certain tree on campus to sit down and just grieve.

While I was sitting there, the students I left in class started heading out of class. One of the students was in my Greek class. He saw me and came to me, for it was unusual for me to leave class early. He approached and called me using a Greek word, *Adelphos*, which means *brother!* He asked me, "What's the matter, and why are you down here by yourself?"

I did not respond to him at the moment because I was truly overwhelmed by the grieving situation. My family was over twelve thousand miles away, and here I was, a stranger in a foreign country, who had just lost his dear sister.

Brother Robert was just a couple steps away from where I was sitting. My face was down, and I was just crying. I did not know what to do other than simply cry to God. When Brother Robert arrived, he tapped on my shoulder and told me, "Brother Nicholas, you will be all right, and things will be fine." Then he asked me, "What's the matter?"

I started to explain to him about the saddest news I had just received. As Brother Robert started comforting me, other students saw us, and they started coming down to where we were, wanting to know what was going on. He explained to them that I had just received a phone call from Kenya, and my sister had passed away.

All of the students surrounded me and started to pray for me and comforted me as I dealt with my loss in a foreign land. Within a twinkling of an eye, I felt support, comfort, and a sense of being surrounded by brothers and sisters in the Lord. It was such a hard time to grieve such a loss in a faraway country. But God had placed His people to render service to Him practically to me at the hour of need.

The college administration and the student body became my big support during my grieving period. That was such a great practical Christianity, which became a necessity and was put to work at the right time in a desperate situation.

This short account is just one among many other stories God's people might be experiencing each day in our churches. They need God's people to put their practical Christianity to work as they minister to God's suffering people. As born-again Christians, we should practice what we have learned in our churches as we minister to people. We should not sit back and watch other people, who have become God's disciples, use their spiritual gifts while we don't do anything to advance God's kingdom. There is a requirement for true disciples of God. When one gives his or her life to the Lord, he becomes a true disciple. No one should let God's people suffer without practicing his or her God-given talent to minister to His people.

Years ago, I was an untrained middle-school teacher before God called me into full-time ministry in Kenya. One day I took twenty students, and I told them, "I will do my best to teach you and train you. If you obey me, you will be the best students of this school."

They were excited. In a short time I realized that only some of them were willing to keep up with my training. Some of them said, "It's too difficult." Some said, "We have more important things to do." Some of them said, "You see other students are having more fun than we do." When they graduated, two of them were the best students of the school. Only two out of twenty.

Jesus was the most extraordinary teacher that ever lived. Jesus Himself had some disciples of the same sort as mine. Some said, "This is a difficult teaching," and they left. He had one disciple who considered money more important than anything. Only a few of them were willing to stay with Jesus until the end. You know why? Because discipleship is difficult; discipleship requires discipline.

We don't like discipline; we want to be free to do whatever we want, to live our lives just as we want. But Christian discipleship requires discipline. I know we are disciples of the Lord, but let me challenge you today to check out your discipleship; be the best disciple you can be.

Jesus was traveling toward Jerusalem followed by crowds of people. He needed disciples to go into villages and cities to preach the message of the kingdom, the fact that the Messiah had come. As Jesus called them out, He shared with them the requirements for true discipleship. As Jesus calls disciples today, the Word of God presents the same requirements for true discipleship.

What are the requirements of true discipleship?

There are three basic requirements for the Christian disciple, as we discover them in the text. True discipleship requires:

1. Mature determination,
2. Prompt submission,
3. Complete devotion.

Now it happened as they journeyed on the road, *that* someone said to Him, "Lord, I will follow You wherever You go."

And Jesus said to him, "Foxes have holes and birds of the air *have* nests, but the Son of Man has nowhere to lay *His* head."

Then He said to another, "Follow Me."

But he said, "Lord, let me first go and bury my father."

Jesus said to him, "Let the dead bury their own dead, but you go and preach the kingdom of God."

And another also said, "Lord, I will follow You, but let me first go *and* bid them farewell who are at my house."

But Jesus said to him, "No one, having put his hand to the plow, and looking back, is fit for the kingdom of God."
—Luke 9:57–62

Luke 9:57–58 tells us that true discipleship requires mature determination.

Matthew 8:19 tells us about a scribe—that is, an intellectual, a theologian, a teacher. He offers himself to follow Jesus, the carpenter, the rabbi from Nazareth. He says, "I will follow you wherever [this is literally *anywhere*] you go."

Now, Jesus makes a very interesting statement: "Foxes have holes and the birds of the air have nests, but the Son of Man has nowhere to lay His head." What is He talking about? Jesus is simply saying, "Discipleship is more difficult than you think. If you really want to be my disciple, count the cost."

There are people who imagine that the Christian life is fun, a lifelong amusement, but it is not. It is a lifelong commitment, through many trials, difficult situations, dangers, persecutions, suffering, and even death, if necessary. You see the birds in the sky. They are free to fly, to sing, to eat, or sleep. Many years ago, one evangelical church in Africa was not allowed to sing! There were Christians who were put in prisons because of their commitment to sing for the Master Jesus. What Jesus is saying is, "If you really want to follow me, count the cost."

Discipleship requires mature determination, such as firmness and boldness that neither "tribulation, or persecution, or famine, or nakedness, or peril, or sword" are able to separate you from your Master (see Rom. 8:35–39).

As a Christian, are you ready, for the sake of Jesus, to leave everything behind—any position, any provision, any possession, any pretension—and follow Him anywhere, with mature determination? Are you totally determined to follow Him literally anywhere? I know we desire to be the pastors in large churches, in important cities, to have our staff, our office, a good car, and a good salary. Are you determined to leave all this and to follow Jesus wherever He leads you? That is what true discipleship really means. This is the first requirement of Christian discipleship,

The second requirement of true discipleship is prompt submission.

The second man had an extraordinary chance: Jesus takes the initiative and offers him an invitation: "Follow me."

But this man replies, "Let me first go and bury my father!"

I don't know if his father was dead or not. Probably the man was asking for permission to go and stay with his father until he died. The text doesn't say exactly what he meant. What I know is that he failed to submit to the Lord right then. He put himself first, and he put his personal and family affairs before his calling.

Earlier, I said that Jesus was an extraordinary teacher. What an interesting response He gives in verse 60: "Let the dead bury their own dead." That really means, "Let the spiritually dead bury the physically dead. Let those who are dead in their sins bury the dead in their homes. Your divine responsibility in the kingdom of God is much higher than any human, family, or social responsibility. You go and preach."

There is an old tradition in our schools in Kenya. When a teacher comes into a classroom, all of the students are standing and waiting for the teacher to sit down. Then they sit, and from that moment on, for the rest of the class period, the teacher is in charge of the hour. The teacher is the master, and the student is required to submit to the teacher's authority. When the teacher asks something, no student will say, "Let me first do something else." He will submit promptly and entirely.

How much more a Christian disciple must promptly submit to the greater authority of our Lord and Savior Jesus Christ. In Christian discipleship there is no room for "Let me first do what I want to do, or go to where I want to go, or say what I want to say." The Christian disciple knows to say right at the beginning of his prayer, "Thy kingdom come, Thy will be done!"

Please check again your discipleship. Are you willing to submit promptly to Jesus, even before other human responsibilities? Are you ready to sacrifice your day off and visit the needy? Is the kingdom of God more important for you than fishing or hunting or playing or sleeping? What are your priorities? Are submission and obedience your strong points? If so, you are a disciple of Jesus.

The third man is a combination of the first and the second: he is a volunteer, like the first one. "I will follow you, Lord," but he uses the same phrase as the second one. "But let me first ..." To him, Jesus addresses a third requirement for Christian discipleship:

True discipleship requires complete devotion.

"Let me first go and say goodbye to my family." This is a perfectly logical desire. Why was Jesus so harsh on the man when he was asking for just a small favor?

Jesus knew his heart, and he said, "No one, having put his hand to the plow, and looking back, is fit for the kingdom of God" (v. 62). In other words, "If you want to be a true disciple, don't let other things hinder you; you'd better devote yourself completely to the kingdom."

Some people in Africa are still using this primitive method to plow the ground. The plowman has to hold the handle of the plow and drive it straight ahead, he has to drive the oxen, and he has to avoid rocks and bushes that could break the plow. A plowman would not look back while plowing for three reasons: (1) The plowing is the first major activity in the field; it is very important to do it in time and properly; (2) There is no time to look around. The day is short, the job is demanding, so he'd better devote himself completely to the task; (3) The plow is expensive; he cannot afford to break the plow.

Jesus said that we cannot do two things at the same time, serve God and serve mammon (Matt. 6:24). We cannot love God and love the world (James 4:4). We have to be single-track-minded. How many ministers are "breaking the plow," destroying their ministries, their families, and themselves, by turning their attention from the Lord to the world, or to money, or to immoral sexual pleasures?

Discipleship is too important to be done halfheartedly, without complete devotion. Remember the Old Testament commandment, to "love the LORD your God with all your heart, with all your soul, and with all your strength" (Deut. 6:5). That means complete devotion.

We have seen three people and three requirements:

1. Mature determination,
2. Prompt submission,
3. Complete devotion.

Many years ago, a university professor decided to resign from his job. Nobody was able to change his mind—not his mother, nor his friends, nor his colleagues. The professor was determined, and nothing was able to stop him.

Some months later, a former colleague met him and asked him: "How are you doing? What is your new job?"

"I am a mail carrier," he said. "And, yes, I like it. The only problem I have is that I am too slow. My postmen colleagues are able to finish their task two or three hours earlier than me. You see, whenever I have to deliver the mail to an old lady, I stop at her door to ask her how she is doing, what she needs, and how I can help her. Often she really needs someone to talk to. I stop to listen to her and to encourage her. Sometimes I feel compelled to sit with an old deserted man. I read two or three verses from the Bible, I pray with him, then I go. Sometimes, while distributing the newspapers, I share the good news. The day is too short to do what I need to do."

"Are you sure this is what you want to do?"

"Oh, yes," the postman said. "In fact, this is what my Master wants me to do, and I love it ..."

I think this is an example of discipleship, to be in God's business with determination, submission, and devotion.

God challenges us today to commit ourselves as true disciples. Probably you say, "I don't know if I can. I'm not sure if I could live my good life in this country, with my family, my friends, my habits." If you can't, then you are not a true disciple, but you can become one. Do it God's way.

I hope that by reading this book you would hear today the sweet call of Jesus, "Follow me." Don't turn away. Respond to God today and be a true disciple. Each Christian is supposed to grow in his walk with God. He or she is required to mature spiritually. He would do so by studying the Word of God as a spiritual diet in his life. He surely will grow spiritually and be willing to apply what he has learned to minister to others who are in need or are struggling.

First Peter 2:1–3 tells us about the importance of Christian spiritual growth: "Therefore, laying aside all malice, all deceit, hypocrisy, envy, and all evil speaking, as newborn babes, desire the pure milk of the word, that you may grow thereby, if indeed you have tasted that the Lord is gracious."

Seven years ago, my wife and I took our youngest son for a regular physical check-up, and the doctor told us, "Everything is fine with him, except his growth. Last time he was doing fine; now he is thinner. What does he eat?"

We said, "He prefers to eat candies and ice cream, not healthy food."

The doctor said, "Put aside all the junk food. Give him milk, bread, meat, and vegetables."

Do you know that a Christian must have a spiritual diet? I was blessed to discover it in 1 Peter, chapter 2. I like Peter. Peter is quite often pictured in the pages of Scripture as eating or sitting at the table. Here, in chapter 2, he is not referring material food, but spiritual food by which a Christian may grow up in his or her spiritual life.

Probably you know some particular Christians who are very weak, thin, and narrow in their Christian life. They have no power to stand up for Christ, they have no power to go and accomplish their mission, no nerve, no joy, no energy. Perhaps you are that kind of Christian. You have to adjust your spiritual diet.

In 1 Peter 2:3, the apostle Peter builds up the whole passage on this condition. If you have tasted the kindness of God, then verses 1 and 2 are for you. If you know God personally, then the spiritual diet is for you.

- There is no human being who has never tasted God's kindness. His kindness is seen in His creation, in His care, in the rain over all, in His protection, in His provision, and in everything that surrounds us.
- There is no Christian who has never tasted God's kindness and love revealed to us in the person and *work* of Jesus Christ.

Consequently, this brief word is for you. First of all, because you have tasted the kindness of God, and secondly, because you need to grow. Verse 2 tells us that this diet is for growth.

Peter wrote this passage so that its receivers might know that Christians are supposed to grow through a spiritual diet. What are the specific characteristics of a spiritual diet? The text reveals two basic characteristics of a spiritual diet. The spiritual diet excludes worldly food. If you want to grow, you have to exclude from your spiritual diet all unhealthy worldly, sinful food.

The apostle presents five specific sins that Christians must eliminate from their lives. It is very interesting that the Bible refers to these sins by the means of food:

1. Wickedness, the anger that boils deep in the heart. First Corinthians 5:8 tells us that there is a leaven of wickedness; a Christian should not celebrate the feast with this sinful food.
2. Guile, literally the bit of food that a fisherman puts on his hook to catch fish. It is a means to catch others; I give you a Christmas gift so that you may give me a Christmas gift.
3. Hypocrisy. Do you remember what the leaven of the Pharisees is? Hypocrisy. Again, it is a food. In that time,

actors were called hypocrites; "I love you brother, I wish I never met you."

4. Envy, jealousy, resentment, rivalry. Proverbs 23:6 says, "Do not eat the bread of a miser, nor desire his delicacies."

5. Slander, which is, literally, backbiting; when someone is telling you something about your neighbor. "The words of a talebearer are like tasty trifles" (Prov. 18:8).

This is a bad food. You'd better stay away from it. It hinders your growth.

But you know everybody does it. This is the food that everybody enjoys.

The most difficult thing in a diet is discipline. Do you remember Daniel? The king's meal was for everybody, but not for him and for his friends. They had another food to eat.

The Christian diet requires discipline, to be willing to put aside all evil habits, all wrong feelings, all sinful acts. Perhaps you see deep in your heart anger or perfidy, or hypocrisy, or jealousy, or calumny. You cannot grow "in respect to salvation" unless you put them aside, unless you throw them out of your life. Confess and forsake them and ask to be cleansed by the blood of Jesus. The next time Satan comes with similar stuff, reject him. Your growth depends on what you receive in your heart.

The spiritual diet is based on spiritual food, i.e., the Word of God. First Peter 2:2 says, "Desire the pure milk of the word." If a Christian is to grow, then he or she must grow with the Word of God. This is the right food for the soul. There are several things to be mentioned here:

1. A Christian is supposed to absorb the Word of God. Not novels, nor books—not even religious books—nor videotapes, TV, or radio, but primarily the pure Word of God.

2. The Christian is supposed to long for the Word, systematically, just as a newborn baby longs for milk. Not weekly, but daily.

3. The Word of God must be absorbed unaltered; not milk and sugar, not milk and honey, but pure milk. Many Christians alter the true meaning of the Bible by adding sweet human doctrines so that it might accord with their desires. They say, "God is good, He will understand …"

4. The Word is profitable to grow in respect to salvation. We are supposed to grow after being saved, not remain baby Christians, but to grow.

Some people have children. Do you remember the time when they were newborn babies? How eager they were to suck milk, to be fed. Five times a day, pure material milk. That's good for growth. In the same manner, the Word of God is good for Christian growth. We need to take it regularly, systematically, and abundantly. The base of the Christian diet is the Word of God.

Let me ask you these questions: Are you hungry for the Word of God? Do you enjoy reading, memorizing, studying, and meditating on the Word of God? Is the Word of God the greatest pleasure you have? Is it more precious than gold to you? Your spiritual well-being depends on your daily feeding with the Word of God.

I used to know a man in Kenya. He was not trained; he didn't even have a high-school education. He was simply a believer. His only joy was to study the Bible and to serve God. His wisdom was well known among Christians. When he went to be with the Lord some years ago, he knew the Holy Bible word for word, even the punctuation, and he was able to wisely apply it in every situation. How is that possible?

He continuously fed himself with spiritual food from the Word of God. Every day he took out the Bible from his pocket and filled his mind with the Word. It is no wonder to me that he knew his Bible so well.

Perhaps you say, "I don't know if I can." Let me tell you, Peter's teaching is positive; you can. God's power is sufficient in our weakness. Our problem is that we don't take time to know God, to taste Him. We lack discipline, and we find books, TV, or the Internet more interesting than the Word of God.

I challenge you today to a new life, to grow up in Christ. If you have tasted "the kindness of the Lord," then this word from apostle Peter is for you. Put aside your sinful actions and reactions and take the Word of God as your spiritual food, and you will grow.

As you read this chapter, if you haven't yet tasted the kindness of God, let me challenge you today to look at the cross. In the person, suffering, death, and resurrection of Jesus Christ we have the most extraordinary revelation of God's kindness. Put your trust in Jesus. Ask forgiveness for your sins, and begin today a new life with Him.

Discussion Questions

- Do you believe that Christians should be engaged practically in serving God faithfully in the church?

- If you do, what measures have you taken to encourage your fellow Christian brothers and sisters in the Lord to be engaged in this way?

- Are you personally involved fully in serving God in your church?

- Can you testify that you have been blessed to minister to someone in your life?

- How does it make you feel when you volunteer in your church to help at vacation Bible school?

- How much joy do you see on the faces of those children attending vacation Bible school?

- Are you willing to reach out to another person in your church or another church to be involved in vacation Bible school?

- Do you see a senior citizen in your church whom you can personally encourage by doing something good for them?

- Do you know that doing acts of kindness to others is a blessing to you from God?

- Do you believe that all people, whether believers or nonbelievers, deserve our love and prayers as well as acts of kindness?

- If you do, what steps have you personally taken to reach out to them?

CHAPTER 7 ～๑

THE HEART OF A SHEPHERD

THE MAASAI PEOPLE are cattle keepers. They start training their children at the age of four years regarding how to be good shepherds of the flock. When their children reach the age of six, they are ready to take the goats to the pasture by themselves. They know how to take the goats to the good grazing pasture. Since the Maasai have great experience in being shepherds, they know when one of their flock is suffering from a certain disease. They truly show off their skills as they take care of their flock. The Maasai elders are the chief shepherds to their flock. They provide security, they refer their sick flock for a veterinary check-up, and they make sure all of the animals are washed and groomed. The Maasai elder has the heart of a shepherd.

God is always our Good Shepherd who continues to take care of His people. Day and night, He provides for us and makes sure we are safe and secure. On many occasions, God has proved to all of us that we belong to Him and He is our Shepherd. There is nothing impossible with our God. He truly has a big heart as a shepherd.

Many years ago in Europe, there was a great plague that killed one third of the population. It was called the black plague. Tens of thousands were killed each and every month, and the population was terrified by the thought of facing death in their families and homes. No one knew who would be the next to die. Many Europeans who were able to go to a safer place did so.

There was a man in England whose family left the country to go to a better place. They persuaded him to come there, otherwise he would be condemned to die by the plague, they said. This man didn't feel peace to leave like that, and he asked them to give him a day to decide. He knew the situation. He knew that if he stayed, he would possibly be on death row. He knew that his decision would be the most important in his life. In a way, he had to decide whether to live or die.

After a long time of prayer, he took his Bible, and he read a few verses as the Bible opened to him. Amazingly enough, the text he read was Psalm 91:5–7.

> You shall not be afraid of the terror by night, nor of the arrow that flies by day, nor of the pestilence that walks in darkness, nor of the destruction that lays waste at noonday. A thousand may fall at your side, and ten thousand at your right hand: but it shall not come near you.

He took these words by faith and he didn't leave the country. He continued to minister to the dying around him, and he lived during the plague and after that.

Is this not a true testimony that the "Word of God is living and powerful," and that "all God's promises are Yes and Amen?" Is not our God an awesome God? Who is like Him? Who can guard or shepherd like Him? Who is as loving as He is? The whole Bible is full of promises that God will protect, guard, shepherd, keep, and will send His angels to encamp around those who love and fear Him.

How important is it to be sure that whatever is going to happen, you are under God's protection? Human life is short and full of dangers; spiritual life is internal and much more jeopardized by spiritual evil powers. Who is your guard or shepherd? The author of Psalm 121 demonstrates in a beautiful poetic passage that there is no better guard or shepherd than God.

Three times a year, every Jewish man was required to attend sacred worship at the temple in Jerusalem. Larger numbers of people from all over Palestine, in long caravans of pilgrims, leaving their homes and towns, made the tiresome trip up to Jerusalem. Over the mountain range's steep paths, with wild beasts and robbers hiding in ravines and gorges, the pilgrims moved toward Jerusalem, the sacred city where Yahweh dwells in His temple. It has been said that Psalm 121, along with the other fourteen "Psalms of ascent," was sung on the way to Jerusalem. This particular psalm was probably sung as an encouragement in the narrow and heavy path, in the expectance of getting close to God's temple. What strong confidence in God's protection does this psalm reveal?

I'm sure you know that we have a long way to travel. We do not have to travel to Jerusalem to meet God. God is ever-present near us, even in our hearts. Our spiritual pilgrimage is directed toward heaven on a way opened by Jesus, our Lord and Savior. Many difficulties, trials, temptations, and dangers are in our way, since Jesus never promised us a smooth path, but one with many troubles.

It may be that as you read this book, you are right now facing deep valleys in your life, difficult times, struggles, and temptations, and you see no solution to your needs. Maybe, as the man in this psalm, you lift up your eyes and look for help in different places. You would like to escape somewhere; you live in fear of your future; you are continuously troubled in your heart. Maybe you try to find someone to rely on, to give you help, to stay with you all the night long and give you protection and comfort. You need someone to guard your body and soul, to stand powerfully between you and your enemies, to be able to protect you day and night.

My dear friend, I've got good news for you today. There is no better guard or shepherd than God. Maybe you say, "How can it be? God is in His heaven; I'm here with my struggles. He is too far from me. Maybe He doesn't care about me. How can I be sure that what you say, or what the psalmist says, is true? Why is God the best guard or shepherd for me?"

Listen to the Holy Spirit of God, and He will reveal to you seven reasons by which you may know that, indeed, the best guard or shepherd for you is God, and in Him you will find much blessing and comfort for your troubled heart.

The author of this Psalm of Ascent expressed in poetry the blessing of having God as a personal guard or shepherd. The believer enjoys the blessing of having God as a guard or shepherd. Why it is a blessing to have God as a guard or shepherd? Psalm 121 reveals seven reasons that prove the blessing of having God as a guard or shepherd. When God is our guard, He protects us incomparably, immediately, and powerfully.

Looking at Psalm 121:1–2, we do not know what problem the writer faces, but we do know that he is helpless. He has no resources to solve his problems, he has no one to help him, and he is looking to find help in the mountains. Like most ancients, the Israelites thought of mountains as being the dwelling place of God, especially Mount Sinai and Mount Zion. Mountains also served as dwelling places for people and as places of refuge, fortresses, and hiding places. The author tries to find help in creation, in created things, in matter, and in visible things. (How often we too, longing for help, look for it in things that cannot help us, in our possessions, in our abilities, or even in other human beings that are as helpless as we are.)

But looking in the text to see from whence comes the help, "My help comes from the LORD, who made heaven and earth."

The One able to help is a person, not a thing; is God, not a hill; is the Creator, not a creature; is the Lord, not a place. How much greater help can God provide than a lifeless hill?

Look again to those two instances of the verb "comes." In the Swahili Bible, the first instance is in future tense (from whence will my help come?), and the second is in present tense (my help comes from the LORD). While your help from God is coming, the help from elsewhere is still in the future. God helps you now, when you need Him, not sometime later.

Our God is incomparable in His power, character, concern, and record; He is the Creator of everything.

Many years ago in Kenya, the father of one of my students came to me and told me what God had done for his family. His daughter had been born with a serious physical problem. Doctors said that she would not be able to give birth her entire life. Her father and mother began to pray fervently for their little girl, and after six months they returned to visit the medical team. It was a big surprise for them to realize that now the girl was completely well, with no sickness or infirmity. I do not know how the doctors interpreted this, but, for the parents, it was God's hand that created from nothing the entire reproductive part in the body of their daughter.

It is absolutely normal that God, the Creator of everything, is able to help much more than a piece of creation, a hill, or a man, or anything else. God says that He cannot be compared with anything. He cannot be compared with other gods (Isa. 40:25, "To whom shall I be equal?"). God cannot be compared with anything: He is unique in His power, character, knowledge, grace, love … everything. That is why He can help, incomparably more than anything else.

When you have God as your guard or shepherd, you will not need another to help. Imagine yourself having beside you a guard or shepherd that is declared the most powerful person in the world. Would you still be afraid? Would you try to find help in someone else? God is the most powerful in the whole universe because He is the Creator of the universe. Trust Him and do not try to find help in anything else. He is sufficient for you. Do not trust in your friends, people around you, or your own abilities. Do not trust in your possessions, in your guns, or in your money, but trust in the Lord. Let Him be your guard or shepherd. He will provide an incomparable help for you.

When God is our guard or shepherd, He protects us diligently: in our walk and sleep.

Looking at verse 3 of Psalm 121, we see reference to the sliding of the foot, frequently used to describe misfortune. It is a very natural occurrence in mountainous Canaan, where a single slip of the foot could bring great danger. This expression refers not only to the foot, but also to the whole body, the entire being. God is interested in your well-being, in your safety, and that your footing would be on safe places. He will not permit any harm to your being. Is it not marvelous?

And look further—God is watching over you, not only when you walk, but when you sleep too. When you sleep during the night hours, you can rest in peace, for God watches over you. He watches, not slumbering, but diligently.

I remember years ago, my friend from Kenya was in the military, and he told me he had to watch some parts of the barracks for three hours during the night. After a long day with much work, he told me, it was very difficult to stay awake and to watch carefully. He admitted that sometimes he fell asleep, and hoped that the hour would pass quickly so he could go to bed. It was hard to stay awake, he said. His eyelids were heavy, he felt as though he had sand in his eyes, his mind was slow, his thoughts were confused, and his feet were staggering. It was awful.

But this is not true for God. All over the earth, people sleep at different hours, but God watches over them continuously and diligently. God is interested in your sleep. Is that not extraordinary? The Bible teaches us that God watched over Paul through three shipwrecks (see 2 Cor. 11:25)! He kept His loving eyes upon Daniel while in the lion's den, over Jonah in the fish's belly, over Moses in his basket, over Jeremiah in prison. You are as precious as they are in the sight of the Lord, and He promises to be your guard or shepherd, just as He was a guard and shepherd to them.

Maybe you are passing right now through a difficult situation, through a narrow path full of dangers. Do not be afraid—the Lord will not allow your foot to be moved. Even in the darkest hour, He does not sleep, He does not even close His eyes as human beings do. He is God, not man. He can protect you; He will guard you with a father's diligence. You are precious in His sight. Take courage, do not be afraid to close your eyes to sleep. He will lovingly look upon you while you take your rest, as a mother or father enjoys looking for their children while they sleep. No one can guard and shepherd you as diligently as God does. Trust Him.

When God is our guard and shepherd, He protects us all-inclusively, us and our dear ones.

Years ago, I traveled to a new church to preach in Kenya. On my way to this church, which was in the Maasai jungle in the middle of nowhere, I prayed that God would protect my family when I was gone, and God was faithful to do so. Not only my close family was kept by the Lord, but also my extended family, all of my relatives, my friends, my former students, my home church—all of them were guarded by God. And not only that, but my nation was also under God's protection for the sake of His elect.

This psalm has a stair-like structure (a common characteristic of the psalms of ascent). In stair-like fashion, the phrases are in an ascending structure; the thought of the first line is repeated and emphasized at the beginning of the second line. Looking in verse 4, we see that the Lord not only guards you and shepherds you, but He is also the keeper of Israel.

This thought must have been very dear to the Jewish traveler. He was on his way toward Jerusalem, but his family was miles away; he had no chance to know what was going on there nor a chance to protect them. The many dangers a family could face in that time and setting included wild beasts, enemies, and emergency situations. The author suggests, "Do not be afraid. The Lord who is your guard and shepherd is Israel's guard and shepherd too; your family is not in danger."

It was a time when all the men in the nation were away to worship God in His temple. What would happen if the Philistines or the Moabites or the Ammonites came to strike their families during the men's worship festivals? There was no need to fear: God would protect Israel. He keeps Israel and, as it is true for you that He will not sleep nor slumber, it was true for Israel too. God is so interested in those with whom He has a special relationship by grace that He will protect their families, cities, and nations.

God is able and willing to guard and shepherd those who cannot guard their families while gone on long trips for a few weeks. You cannot protect yourself, nor them. But God can guard and shepherd you and your family. Do you remember what Elisha said to his servant when Samaria was surrounded by an army with horses and chariots? "Do not fear," he said, "for those who are with us are more than those who are with them" (2 Kings 6:16). The Lord was a guard and shepherd for Samaria and Israel that day.

Sometimes it is hard to be gone and not to worry about your family, or even your nation. It is difficult to be a Christian or a

Jew and have no fear for the sake of Israel. There is no need to fear. God is the keeper. He will guard and shepherd you, and them as well. Being powerless in issues too big for us is not a reason to worry. We have a mighty God who is our God, and our nation's guard and shepherd too. Praise to Him. There is something more the psalm says about God as our guard and shepherd ...

When God is our guard and shepherd, He protects us continually, day and night.

In verses 5 and 6 of Psalm 121, we see a contrast to the variable climatic conditions experienced in many parts of North America and the conditions in Israel that, during the summer months, are relatively stable. Warm days and cooler nights are the rule in Israel, and it almost never rains. In Jerusalem, for example, the average August daytime high temperature is 86 degrees Fahrenheit; the nighttime average low is 64 degrees Fahrenheit. Israel is one of the sunniest countries in the world.

Everybody understands what it means to get sunstroke. But how can the moon strike you? The influence of the moon was considered by the Eastern people to be very dangerous, in hot climates especially. The name given to persons of disordered intellect, *lunatic,* arose from the widespread belief of the effect of the moon on those who were exposed to its influence. The idea here is that God is your guard and shepherd day and night, and there is no natural law able to affect negatively God's protégé. You can have full confidence in God's protection.

Imagine yourself traveling with Israelites through the desert toward Canaan. The sun strikes you right on the top of your head. The sun shines, and your eyes are red and tired of the view. There is no shelter to sit under, and no shadow, no oasis. But God has something special for you: a cloud to shade you. And during the night, in the deepest darkness, in coolness, God has a pillar of fire to show you that He is there, never forsaking you. You can roll over and continue your sleep. God is there, your guard and shepherd at the door of your camp.

This is true not only for Israel, but this is true for us too. The Lord has promised that He will guard and shepherd us continually, day and night. Remember what our dear Savior told His disciples right before He left for heaven: "Lo, I am with you always, even to the end of the age" (Matt. 28:20). The confidence that our Lord is with us in every situation, every time, day and night, fills our hearts with joy and faith.

My beloved fellow saints, do you realize that God cares so much for us that He guards and shepherds us continuously, and He protects us from every harm that might fall upon us? In your darkest hour, in your most difficult problem, just look at your right side. Find there the shadow and remember that you are not alone. Very close to you, right at your right hand, God is shadowing you so that nothing can harm. Trust Him: He is guarding and shepherding you.

When God is our guard and shepherd, He will protect us entirely—body and soul.

In verse 6, God guards your body from natural evil influences. Verse 7 adds a new dimension of God's protection: He guards and shepherds your soul from all evil, that is, from evil spiritual influences. The Hebrew word *nepesh,* soul, can be translated in different ways: *breath, respiration, life, soul, spirit, mind, creature, person, self.* The term can also be translated as *heart,* i.e., the inner man. It is clear that the text refers to God's protection for the whole person: body, and soul. There are many ways to preserve the soul from evil. The soul is kept by God from the dominion of sin, the infection of error, the puffing up of pride, the world, the Devil.

In Kenya, as elsewhere, military buildings are very important. Permanent teams guard the buildings and all properties of the army so that no enemy will come in and destroy or steal our secrets. But the most precious thing in a military building is the flag of that military unit. Apart from the guards outside the building, there is a permanent guard inside the building that watches day and night to protect the flag. The moment the flag is stolen or destroyed, that unit ceases to exist.

The human soul is the invisible, immaterial part of man, the very heart of the person. Jesus said that our souls are more important than our bodies, and the soul is more valuable than the whole world (Ps. 35:9; Luke 1:46–47; Luke 12:4–7). Psalm 121 assures me that the Lord guards and shepherds not only the external, material, visible part of our self, but the inner, immaterial, invisible part also. Is it not marvelous that God is the guard and shepherd of the most precious part of a human being, the soul? He shall preserve it from all evil. What a precious assurance.

Indeed, He can do that. Paul's prayer for the Thessalonian church was that the "whole spirit and soul and body be preserved blameless at the coming of our Lord Jesus Christ" (1 Thess. 5:23). When Jesus died on the cross, He committed His soul into the hands of the Father, and so did Stephen. Why so? Because God can guard and shepherd the soul, and His protection is much stronger than any evil attempt to destroy it. But God is able to guard and shepherd your soul not only in death, but also in daily life to protect it from all dangers.

You may feel sometimes that your soul is weak and you cannot stand against the Devil's attacks through bad thoughts, sadness, discouragement, temptations, and hurtful feelings. Maybe you think you are too sinful to be forgiven or you look around you and see only hypocrites, and Satan is piercing you with many evils. Look up to the Lord and claim His protection. He is able to guard and shepherd you. "Resist the devil and he will flee from you" (James 4:7). Be strong in the Lord. He will preserve your soul and your body too.

In June 2010, my wife and I and another pastor and his wife and three young adults traveled to Kenya for a two-week mission trip. As I led this trip, I was praying each day and night that all would be well and safe. The team had never traveled to Africa before, and all were excited. But in my heart, I was somehow nervous because traveling nowadays is very scary. The journey was safe, and all of us arrived safely in Nairobi. We met our host pastors waiting for us, and our transportation team was ready to take us to the mission field. In my heart was a concern for the safety of the team and their health for the two weeks we were to stay over there. But God proved to me that it was not I who was in charge of the team, but God Himself. He guarded and shepherded us and protected us tremendously. None of us were ever sick, not even scratched by anything on our bodies. We all returned to the United States well and healthy.

Do you realize that through this stair-like structure, the Holy Spirit takes us upward, step by step, and He fills our hearts with joy as we read through this psalm? The Lord not only protects our bodies and souls, but He is also interested in our daily work and our daily activities.

When God is our guard and shepherd, He protects us extensively—here and everywhere.

I remind you that this psalm was to be sung on special occasions, in the procession going up to Jerusalem for annual worship. The men were far away from their homes. Their concern was to spend a few days worshipping in God's temple and then to return home to continue their daily activities until the next time when they would go out again on their journeys and also on their next trip. He would protect them in their walk, not just for religious duties, but in their domestic affairs too. The Lord God would guard and shepherd them as they traveled, worked ... everywhere. It is good to know that the Lord is our guard and shepherd, not only in the worship place, but outside it too. He is our protector, not only on Sundays, but on weekdays too.

My ancestors were farmers and shepherds. Their tasks were varied and arduous, demanding and dangerous. Not only did they have to protect their sheep from dangers, sickness, and wild beasts, but they also had to be constantly searching for good pastures and sufficient water. I remember when my grandfather taught me how to tend to the flock. Every morning he took them out to the streams of water and then to good pastures. When the day was toward evening, he led them back to water and then to the stable. Every morning and every evening he counted them diligently, and he rejoiced that he did not lose any of them.

Just like that, I imagine God lovingly guarding and shepherding us in the morning when we go out to our workplaces, all during the day, and in the evening when we return home. We'll never know how many dangers surround us daily, but God protects us carefully.

The Lord can protect our going out and coming in, just because He is God. He can watch over us completely and for countless times. He is not restricted in space. He can be in Jerusalem in His temple and, at the same time, He can watch over your family in Beer-Sheba, Hebron, or Jericho. He can guard and shepherd you here and everywhere. He is never absent. Even in the deep water, He is there; even in the depths of the earth, He is there. Is this not great joy? The God of the universe is willing to guard and shepherd you all the day long, everywhere you go.

Each Sunday, we rejoice in God's presence in His church. Does He go home with us? Sure, He does! The next day, we start a new week. We leave our beds early in the morning, and we return late in the evening. Our daily tasks lead us to many places. Does He go with us and bring us safely home? Sure, He does! But we are many; even in a home, the father goes in a direction, the mother in another direction, the kids will take other directions. Does God go with us all? Sure, He does! Is that not marvelous? What a marvelous God we have!

Now the staircase is almost climbed. What else has the psalm to say in addition to what it has already said? Can there be something more exciting? Oh, yes, there can.

When God is our guard and shepherd, He protects us endlessly—now and forever.

This sentence is the climax; here the confidence in God reaches the ultimate in assurance. The worshipper can leave the sanctuary and enter the realm where he faces danger in rugged mountains, under the burning sun, and the threat of many dangers, but he may be sure that God's protection is everlasting, eternal. The expression used here means endless time, indefinite future, continually without change, and ever-continuing. The Lord will guard and shepherd His own in the present and in the future—endlessly.

My daughter told me one day that she wished that we would never be separated. She doesn't want to stay with other people, only with Mom and Dad and young siblings. She said one time that she would not get married, for she wants us to be with her forever. But we know this is not possible. The time will come when she will be in school, with neither Dad nor Mom beside her. The day will come when she will (gladly) say goodbye, and she will stay with her husband and not with her parents. The time will come when we as parents will be done with our role of raising her.

But, you know what? God will never leave us! Tomorrow He will be at the same place, at the right hand, and the day after tomorrow, and next week, and next year, and in the last hour too, and forevermore. Is that not exciting?

His Word is full of encouragement, such as this verse I am going to give you. This word is precious to me: "Listen to me, O house of Jacob, and all the remnant of the house of Israel, who have been borne by Me from birth, and have been carried from the womb: Even to your old age, I will be the same, and even to your graying years I will bear you! I have done it, and I will carry you; and will bear you and I will deliver you" (Isa. 46:3–4 NASB). And also how precious is Jesus' promise that I already quoted that He will be with us always, "even to the end of the age."

My dear fellow saints in Christ, rejoice in the Lord, He will not leave us, nor forsake us, because he says "I have inscribed you on the palms of My hands"(Isa. 49:16 NASB). Do not be afraid of tomorrow or of your older years. There is one who will never leave you, from now on and even forevermore. How blessed we are to have God as our guard and shepherd!

I remember one time driving on a completely unknown route. It was dark, early in the morning, just after midnight. I didn't know the way, and I thought I could drive ahead and somehow would find the town I was looking for. It was the time when all the routes in Kenya were very poorly signalized—no lights, no signs, and no marks. Suddenly, I had a feeling that I must stop right there and get out of the car to check the route. I realized later that this was God's voice. I stopped the car right there and got out. Trying to discern through the dark, I understood why God had told me to stop. A foot away, in front of my car, was a huge ditch. I was so glad I had God as my guard and shepherd.

There is a blessing to having God as your protector. No one can guard and shepherd you as He does. He guards and shepherds you diligently, in your walk, and even in your sleep. He protects you and your dear ones. He watches over you continuously, day and night, entirely, body and soul. He guards and shepherds you completely, here and everywhere. He promises to guard and shepherd you now and for all eternity

What an amazing guard and shepherd we have in God! Trust Him! Worship Him now! Serve Him in His ministry with others, and advance His kingdom as we wait for His return! Leave with

Him in the morning, in your daily walk, and come back with Him at night! Walk with Him now and forever! Amen.

Discussion Questions

- Do you believe that God is the greatest Shepherd of all?
- If you do, what have you done to make sure all of your friends know about this great Shepherd?
- Do you acknowledge the power of this great Shepherd?
- Do you believe that God began his shepherding in your life before you were born?
- Do you honor Him because of all He has done for you and your family?
- Do you ever doubt whether God is the greatest Shepherd who ever lived?
- Would you encourage your friends to believe in this great Shepherd?
- If you would, what strategy would you be willing to use?
- Are you convinced that this Shepherd has protected many people?
- Do you think there will ever be any other shepherd stronger than God?
- Has He proved to be the only One we will ever know and believe?
- Who else can try to challenge this great Shepherd?
- Do you think this other challenger can defeat this Shepherd you believe in?

NOTES

Alexander, David, and Pat Alexander *Eerdmans' Handbook to the Bible*. Grand Rapids, Michigan: William B. Eerdmans Publishing Company, 1983.

Alexander, J. A. *The Psalms*. Vol. 3. New York: Charles Scribner & Co, 1868.

Anderson, A. A. *The Book of Psalms*. Vol. 2. Oliphants, 1972.

Arndt, William F. *Bible Commentary, The Gospel According to St. Luke*. Saint Louis, Missouri: Concordia Publishing House, 1956.

Barnes, Albert. *Notes on the Old Testament*. Psalms. Vol. 2. Grand Rapids, Michigan: Baker Book House, 1950.

Berry, George Ricker. *The Interlinear Literal Translation of The Greek New Testament*. Grand Rapids, Michigan: Zondervan Publishing House, 1976.

Brown, Francis. *The New Brown-Driver-Briggs-Gesenius Hebrew and English Lexicon*. Christian Copyrights, Inc, 1983.

Bullock, C. Hassel. *An Introduction to the Old Testament Poetic Books*. Chicago: Moody Press, 1988.

Barker, Kenneth L, and John R. Kohlenberger III. *The Expositor's Bible Commentary: Old Testament.* Grand Rapids, Michigan: Zondervan, 1994.

Bonnet, Kenneth. "Briefs from Around Southeastern." *Outlook: The Magazine of Southeastern Baptist Theological Seminary,* October 2011: 28.

Carlisle, Richard, ed. *The Illustrated Encyclopedia of Mankind.* Vol. 10. Londan, 1974. Cash, W.D. *The Mind of The South.* New York: Alfred A. Knoff, 1941.

Clarke, Arthur G. *Analytical Studies in the Psalms.* Kansas City: Walterick Publishers, 1967.

Croft, Steven J. L. *The Identity of the Individual in the Psalms.* Worcester: Sheffield Academic Press, 1987.

Currie, David R. *On The Way.* Nashville, Tennessee: Broadman Press, 1982.

Dahood, Mitchell. *The Anchor Bible, Psalms III.* Garden City, New York: Doubleday & Company, Inc., 1970.

Delitzsch, Franz. *Biblical Commentary on the Psalms. Vol. 3.* Grand Rapids, Michigan: WM. B. Eerdmans Publishing Company, 1970.

Dockery, David S., Kenneth A. Matthews, and Robert B. Sloan. *Foundations for Biblical Interpretation.* Nashville: Broadman & Holman Publishers, 1994.

Dutchie, Charles S. *God in His World.* New York: Abingdon Press, 1945.

Edgemon, Roy T. *Disciple-All: A Discipleship Training Manual.* Nashville, Tennessee: Convention Press, 1990.

Evans, Craig A. *New International Bible Commentary,* Luke. Peabody, Massachusetts: Hendrickson Publishers, 1990.

Ewald, Heinrich A. *Commentary on the Psalms. Vol. 2.* London: Williams and Norgate, 1881.

Exell, Joseph S. *The Biblical Illustrator, The Psalms. Vol. 5.* Grand Rapids, Michigan: Baker Book House, 1960.

Franklin, John Hope. *History of Racial Segregation in the United States: Racial Segregation and Integration.* 1946.

Freedman, David Noel. *The Anchor Bible Dictionary. Vol. 5.* New York: Doubleday, 1992.

Geisler, Norman L.; Nix, William E. A *General Introduction to the Bible.* Revised and Expanded. Chicago: Moody Press, 1986.

Gooding, David. *According to Luke, A New Exposition of the Third Gospel.* Downer's Grove, Illinois: InterVarsity Press, 1987.

Guthrie, Donald. *New Testament Introduction.* Downers Grove, Illinois: InterVarsity Press, 1990.

Hastings, James. *Encyclopedia of Religion and Ethics.* Edited by Charles Schriners. Vol. 8. New York, 1915.

Henry, Carl F. *The Evangelical Pulpit.* Grand Rapids, Michigan: William B. Eerdmons Publishing Company, 1948.

Hobbs, Herschel H. *New Testament Evangelism.* Nashville, Tennessee: Convention Press, 1960.

Hodding, Carter. *The Angry Scar.* Garden City, New Jersey: Doubleday and Company, 1959.

Kivengeree, Festo. *When God Moves In Revival.* Wheaton, Illinois: Tyndale House Publishers Inc., 1973.

Kraus, Hans-Joachim. *Theology of the Psalms.* Minneapolis: Augburg Publishing House, 1986.

Lockyer, Herbert. *All The Books and Chapters of the Bible.* Grand Rapids, Michigan: Zondervan Publishing House, 1966.

Lockyer, Herbert. *All The Trades and Occupations of the Bible.* Grand Rapids, Michigan: Zondervan Publishing House, 1973.

Logan, Archie. *Spectacular Magazine,* February 2008.

McLarry, Newman R. *Handbook on Evangelism.* 119: Convention Press, 1965.

McGee, J. Vernon. *Thru the Bible with J. Vernon McGee. Vol. 2.* Nashville: Thomas Nelson Publishers, 1982.

Miller, Madeleine S. and Miller J. Lane. *Harper's Bible Dictionary.* New York: Harper & Brothers, Publishers, 1952.

Miller, Madeleine S., and J. Lane Miller. *Harper's Encyclopedia of Bible Life*. New York: Harper & Row Publishers, 1978.

Mowinckel, Sigmund. *The Psalms In Israel's Worship. Vol. 2*. Nashville: Abingdon Press, 1962.

Neill, Stephen, John Goodwin, and Arthur Dowle. *The Modern Reader's Dictionary of the Bible*. New York: Association Press, 1966.

Olin, T. Binkley. *The Churches and The Social Conscience*. Indianapolis, Indiana: National Foundation Press, 1948.

Page II, Charles R., and Carl A. Volz. *The Land and the Book. An Introduction to the World of Bible*. Nashville: Abingdon Press, 1993.

Perowne, J.J. Stewart. *The Book of Psalms. Vol. 2*. Grand Rapids, Michigan: Zondervan Publishing House, 1976.

Pfeiffer, Charles F. *Baker's Bible Atlas. Revised Edition*. Nashville: Broadman Press, 1973.

Pfeiffer, Charles F. *The Biblical World. A Dictionary of Biblical Archaeology*. Grand Rapids, Michigan: Baker Book House, 1966.

Pinson, William. *The World Topical Bible of Issues and Answers*. Waco, Texas: Word Books Publisher, 1981.

Rassmussen, Carl G. *Zondervan NIV Atlas of the Bible*. Grand Rapids, Michigan: Regency Reference Library, Zondervan Publishing House, 1989.

Rogerson, J. W., and J. W. McKay. *Psalms 101-150*. Cambridge: Cambridge University Press, 1977.

Robinson, James. *Seven Ways I Can Serve The Lord*. Nashville, Tennessee: Broadman Press, 1971.

Schokel, Luis Alonso. *A Manual of Hebrew Poetics*. Roma: Editrice Pontificio Instituto Biblico, 1988.

Spurgeon, C. H. *The Treasury of David. Vol. 6*. New York and London: Funk & Wagnalls Company, 1881.

Strong, James. *Strong's Exhaustive Concordance*. Nashville: Broadman Press, 1979.

The Broadman Bible Commentary. Esther–Psalms. Vol. 4. Nashville: Broadman Press, 1971.

The Broadman Bible Commentary, Vol. 9, Luke – John. Clifton J. Allen, General Editor. Nashville, Tennessee: Broadman Press, 1970.

The Interpreter's Bible. Vol. 4. Nashville: Abingdon Press, 1955.

The Interpreter's Bible, Vol. 8. George Arthur Buttrick, Commentary Editor. New York: Abingdon-Cokesbury Press. Nashville, 1952.

The New Topical Text Book. London: Fleming H. Revell Company, 1897.

Tilson, Everett. *Segregation and The Bible.* Nashville, TN: Abingdon Press, 1958.

Vine, W.E. *Vine's Expository Dictionary of Old & New Testament Words.* Nashville: Thomas Nelson Publishers, 1997.

Von Allmen, J. J. *A Companion to the Bible.* New York: Oxford University, 1958.

Von Allmen, J. J. *Vocabulary of the Bible.* London: Lutterworth Press, 1958.

Weiser, Artur. *The Psalms. A Commentary.* Philadelphia: The Westminster Press, 1962.

Weatherford, W.D. *American Churches and the Negro.* Boston: The Christopher Publishing House, 1957.

Wigram, George V., and Ralph D. Winter. *The Word Study Concordance.* Wheaton, Illinois: Tyndale House Publishers, Inc., 1978.

Williams, Donald M. *The Communicator's Commentary. Psalms 73-150.* Dallas, Texas: Word Books Publisher, 1989.

Young, Robert. *Young's Analytical Concordance to the Bible.* Nashville: Thomas Nelson Publishers, 1982.

Zodiathes, Spiros. *The Hebrew-Greek Key Study Bible.* Nashville. Thomas Nelson Publishers, 1990.

Author Contact Information

email: nicjoyce@juno.com

Follow the Author on his Blog:

http://nicholasmuteti.authorweblog.com/

For International Missions Partnership with needy
Maasai children please visit:

http://childplightke.org/

Ordering my book, *Segregation in Churches,* please visit:

http://www.winepresspublishing.com/

For information on an International Mission Trip to Kenya or
any nation in Africa please send me an
email: nicjoyce@juno.com

WinePressPublishing
Great Books, Defined.

To order additional copies of this book call:
1-877-421-READ (7323)
or please visit our website at
www.WinePressbooks.com

If you enjoyed this quality custom-published book,
drop by our website for more books and information.

www.winepresspublishing.com
"Your partner in custom publishing."

CPSIA information can be obtained at www.ICGtesting.com
Printed in the USA
BVOW072301090613

322761BV00002B/12/P